Advanc

A Year o*f*

"Cameron knows how to captivate an audience; her prose is, by turns, humorous, astute, logical, eloquent, and sincere. . . . anecdotes are consistently memorable, and her analysis of them is often brilliant. Overall, this well-organized book is engaging enough to read quickly but profound enough to savor slowly."
—*KIRKUS REVIEWS* (starred review)

"Donna Cameron's contagious warmth, compelling stories, persuasive logic, and useful advice make this gem a joy to read. After I finished each lovely little chapter, I understood the path to kindness a bit better, my inspiration to keep moving down that path increased, and my resolve to forgive myself and others when we slip into unkindness grew stronger."
—ROBERT SUTTON, Professor, Stanford University, and best-selling author of *The No Asshole Rule* and *The Asshole Survival Guide*

"Just being nice will not be enough to save the civility of today's world. It will take the patience and focus of true and loving kindness. Don't assume you know what is needed or how to do it until you read Donna Cameron's *A Year of Living Kindly*. You will find inspiration for every experience and season of your life."
—JOHN KRALIK, author of *A Simple Act of Gratitude*

"This book will absolutely light your heart on fire for kindness! In *A Year of Living Kindly*, Donna Cameron encourages us to suspend our spectator status and fully embrace what's happening around us. Through collected research and her own wise observations, she generously shows us how to lead fuller lives through kindness."
—NICOLE J. PHILLIPS, author of *Kindness is Contagious* and host of *The Kindness Podcast*

"*A Year of Living Kindly* is not only a beautifully written memoir, it's also an insightful and inspiring guidebook, a fountain of wisdom, and a timely gift to the world. In an era when mean-spiritedness, anger, and polarization are so rampant, Donna Cameron draws from her own lived experience, as well as extensive research in medicine and the social sciences, and demonstrates that being kind is both a challenge and our essential nature, that it makes a real difference in the world, and that it enhances our own health and well-being in the process. Highly recommended."

—SUSAN AVERY STEWART, PhD, MFT, Professor Emerita, Sonoma State University, and author of *Winter's Graces: The Surprising Gifts of Later Life*

"It's irrefutable that being kind—*on purpose*—improves health and wellness. With fifty-two delicious, bite-sized chapters containing actionable examples that help readers weave intentional kindness into their daily lives, you can be sure *A Year of Living Kindly* is a book I'll prescribe to my clients."

—LAURIE BUCHANAN, PhD, holistic health practitioner, life coach, and author of *The Business of Being* and *Note to Self*

"An exquisite thread of compassion and kindness is interwoven throughout Donna Cameron's book, *A Year of Living Kindly*. With beautiful wisdom and utterly clear examples, this book leads the reader to a new understanding of how to make the world a better place for all of us. I will recommend it wherever I go."

—DANNA BEAL, MEd, speaker, coach, and author of *The Extraordinary Workplace: Replacing Fear with Trust and Compassion*

A YEAR of LIVING KINDLY

A YEAR
of
LIVING
KINDLY

Choices That Will
Change Your Life and the
World Around You

DONNA CAMERON

SHE WRITES PRESS

Published September 25, 2018
Printed in the United States of America
Print ISBN: 978-1-63152-479-0
E-ISBN: 978-1-63152-480-6
Library of Congress Control Number: 2018935738

For information, address:
She Writes Press
1563 Solano Ave #546
Berkeley, CA 94707

Interior design by Tabitha Lahr

She Writes Press is a division of SparkPoint Studio, LLC.

Names and identifying characteristics have been changed to protect the privacy of certain individuals.

To Bill Wiederkehr, wherever you are is home.

CONTENTS

THE SEASON OF UNDERSTANDING

I. Barriers to Kindness

II. Resistance to Kindness

III. Opening Our Lives to Kindness

THE SEASON OF CHOOSING

I. The Tools of Kindness

II. Choosing Kindness

III. Dealing with Unkindness

THE SEASON OF BECOMING

I. Challenges to Kindness

II. Creating a Kinder World

III. Living Kindness Every Day: Your Kindness Legacy

Introduction:

The World Could Use More Kindness

Kindness is in short supply these days. It's evident on our highways, in crowded public spaces, in our political discourse, and in social and commercial media. In place of everyday courtesy, we encounter glaring contempt. Gracious acknowledgment has given way to disregard. And where polite conversation or civil debate once reigned, we are blitzed by name-calling, insults, and derision. Outshouting the other guy has become the strategy of the day. It doesn't feel good, and it doesn't feel right.

Beyond not "feeling" good, there's plenty of evidence that the unkindness and incivility that surround us are destructive—to our health, our relationships, our happiness, and even our career success. And there's a mounting body of research showing that kindness improves health and extends longevity, strengthens our relationships, boosts business success, and contributes greatly to our overall happiness. There may be a few bullies and tyrants who scoff at kindness, viewing it as a weakness, but the truth is very much the opposite: kindness is a strength, a superpower that has the capacity to transform lives and change the world.

If there's going to be a change, it's up to us to make it. Creating a kinder world is something we all can do—it doesn't require rallying people or institutions, it's not costly, we can do it anywhere and anytime. It doesn't demand that we be smart or rich, or that we be articulate or outgoing. It only requires that we pay attention, and when we face a choice of how we will respond, we choose kindness.

It sounds simple, and it is simple . . . but it isn't easy. We don't always pay attention to our lives; we often act out of habit or in instant response to a perceived insult or provocation. We all have our own insecurities that propel us to act in ways that aren't always compassionate (or even logical). We get tired, we become impatient, we grow fearful, we see slights when they're real and sometimes when they're not. Let's face it, we're human.

I've always admired kind people. I wanted to be more like them. It seemed to me that they travel through their days with a sort of grace that leaves pleasure and calm in their wake. It just feels good to be in the presence of kind people. Over the years, I repeatedly made a commitment to being kind—sometimes it was even my New Year's resolution. And I was kind—until kind wasn't easy, or wasn't convenient. Until somebody or something pushed my buttons. Until I felt threatened or insecure or inadequate. And then I spoke harshly, or sarcastically, or simply turned my back and pretended not to see that I was passing up an opportunity to enrich someone's day, and maybe even improve the world.

I settled for being nice.

Finally, I said I wanted to walk my own talk. I christened 2015 as my "Year of Living Kindly," and to make it harder to let the commitment fade, I blogged about it weekly and invited people to follow the blog (https://ayearoflivingkindly.com/). During my year of living kindly, I recommitted each day to being a kind person, and each day I learned more about kindness—and about myself. Since there isn't a kindness switch, and I had several decades of self-centered niceness as my fallback behavior, I knew I would fail as much as I succeeded. I told myself, though, that if at the end of the year I was a kinder person, I would have achieved what I set out to do.

As the year ended, I was pleased to recognize that I *was* a kinder person, and that kindness—while not yet my default response in every situation—was something I thought about daily and aspired to continually. I saw that bringing more kindness into my life had changed my life—in both subtle and striking ways. And I also saw that becoming a kind person is a lifetime endeavor, not something I can accomplish in a single year. So, instead of a year of living kindly, I have extended the intention of living kindly for as long as I am on the planet.

This book recounts what I learned during my year of living kindly and what I continue to learn. I've tried to approach kindness as I've tried to approach my life—taking it seriously without taking myself too seriously. I wish I could tell you that kindness has become my permanent setting and that I am always kind. But that's not who I am. I am definitely *kinder*, and I am also happier, and I am committed to kindness, but I still have snarky thoughts, moments of impatience, and instances of obliviousness. I'm not the Dalai Lama or Mother Teresa in word or deed, but my world has changed very much for the better. Whether or not I ever become an unfailingly kind person, I will persist in this effort because the world is in desperate need of more kindness. And one thing I've learned with certainty is that if we are to create a better, safer, and more just world, we will do it through kindness.

Are *you* sometimes discouraged by the absence of courtesy and consideration in today's world? Do you wish people were better able to assume the good in one another and act as if we all matter equally? Do you want to deepen your connection with life and also stand up for positive and constructive interactions among all people? If you share my belief that kindness makes a difference and can ultimately change the world, I invite you to declare your own year of living kindly.

There are fifty-two brief chapters in this book, organized loosely into four seasonal clusters and twelve broad topics. You can approach them as weekly meditations on kindness, read them all in a couple of sittings, or simply open to any chapter and see what resonates for you. Each chapter includes a few "Kindness in Action" ideas to help you think about how to apply the chapter's concepts to your own life. Periodic "check-in" chapters help you assess how and where kindness shows up in your world (and where, perhaps, it doesn't), and set some goals accordingly. Read this book and respond to it in whatever ways feel right for you. There is no wrong way to be genuinely kind. Welcome to the kindness community.

PART ONE:

The Season
of Discovery

I. Understanding Kindness

Chapter 1:

Being Nice Isn't the Same as Being Kind

"Three things in human life are important. The first is to be kind; the second is to be kind; and the third is to be kind."
(Henry James)

Stories of kindness are everywhere . . . if we look for them.

Firefighters in Florida responded to a call about a man who had a heart attack while mowing his lawn during an extreme summer heat wave. After the paramedics attended to him and rushed him to the hospital, several of the firemen stayed behind to finish mowing the lawn and cleaning up the man's yard.

A thirteen-year-old girl in Louisville, Kentucky, saw a young boy being teased and bullied by other boys over his tattered shoes. She grabbed a pair of brand-new Nikes from her closet and gave them to him.

Officers in Manchester, England, responded to a call for help from a local woman, fearing that either she or her ninety-five-year-old husband had fallen or injured themselves. What they found, though, was that Doris and Fred were lonely. The officers set the kettle on to brew and sat down to visit with the elderly couple over a cup of tea.

Kind people go beyond what's expected of them. They go beyond the easy response to offer the best of who they are. They do it without expectation of something in return. They do it because of who and what they are and their vision of the world they want to live in.

Most people would tell you I am a nice person. I was raised to be nice. "Be nice" was one of my mother's frequent mantras— it was repeated along with other instructions that aimed to assure that Connie's daughters never gave the neighbors anything to talk about and also never drew too much attention (good or bad) to themselves or to her. "Sit up straight." "Don't bite your nails." "Be nice." These were the refrains of my childhood.

My mother, while generally nice, was not especially kind. Nice allowed her to keep her distance from most people and avoid connecting or interacting at more than a superficial level. She was almost always civil, but effort and warmth were generally absent for all but the closest friends or relatives, and sometimes even then her kindness was restrained. A string of losses from early childhood on had taught her not to trust or hope for too much, or to set her sights too high. She lived with a deep regard for safety and a persistent fear of more loss. With my mother as my model, I learned to be cautious, reserved, and nice.

But some years ago, I realized that wasn't enough. I wanted to be more than nice. I wanted to abandon lingering fears and set my sights high. I wanted to be kind. There's just something about kind people. By their actions, or sometimes by their mere presence, they make us feel good. They give us hope for the world. To me, being kind meant knowing at the end of each day that I had helped, that I was offering the best of who I am, and that I had perhaps made a difference. And it also meant spending less time looking for threats or failings and more time recognizing abundance and compassion. I saw that my life would matter if, at its end, people said of me, "She was a kind person." I could think of no greater eulogy. So I aspired to be kind, and frequently I was. But just as often, I was impatient, I was snarky, I was judgmental, I was indifferent or simply oblivious.

Being kind—truly kind—is hard. Nice requires little effort. I can be nice while also being indifferent, critical, and even sarcastic. But I can't be *kind* and be any of those things. Being kind means caring. It means making an effort. It means thinking about the impact I'm having in an interaction with someone and endeavoring to make it rich and meaningful—giving them what they need at that exact moment, without worrying about whether I get anything in return. It means letting go of my judgments and accepting people as they are. Kindness requires me to do something my upbringing discouraged—it demands that I reach out and that I take a risk.

Nice doesn't ask too much of us. It isn't all that hard to be nice; in fact, it's easy. It's also benign. Passive. Safe. One can be nice without expending too much energy or investing too much of oneself in others. One can be nice without taking risks. Nice is holding the door, smiling at the cashier; nice may even be dropping a couple of dollars in a homeless person's hand if we do so without looking him in the eye and saying a genuinely caring word. Kind is asking how we can help, offering our hand, jumping in without being asked, and engaging in conversation that goes beyond the superficial. All of these actions have an element of risk: we might be rebuffed, ignored, or disrespected.

Years ago, I had the pleasure of knowing Dr. Dale Turner, author, speaker, theologian, and extraordinarily kind man. He always carried with him and handed out little green cards with two simple words printed on them: "Extend Yourself." I've carried that little card in my wallet and had those two words pinned beside my desk for nearly three decades. It seems to me that the phrase "Extend Yourself" captures the essence of kindness. It also highlights the difference between niceness and kindness.

A life of kindness is not something that I live only when it suits me. I'm not a kind person if I'm kind only when it's easy or convenient. A life of kindness means being kind when it's neither convenient nor easy—in fact, sometimes it might be terribly hard and tremendously inconvenient. *That's when it matters most.* That's when the need is greatest and transformation dances at the edge of possibility. That's the time to take a deep breath and invite kindness to dance.

Upon starting my year of living kindly, I began to recognize just how oblivious I can be at times. When my mind is occupied with work problems or planning for my next meeting or deadline, it is all too easy to neglect greeting my office mates, forget to say a few cordial words to the grocery clerk, or fail to thank my husband for filling my car with gas. I tried to pay more attention to little kindnesses: holding a door for someone or sincerely thanking someone who holds a door for me, offering to help if a colleague seems frazzled, or acknowledging people as I walk by them.

From the outset, I tried to make a conscious effort to do things *kindly* that I once may have done *nicely.* Outwardly, there probably wasn't a lot of difference. In the past, if I chose to give a dollar or two to someone who asked me for money, I would do so quickly and hurry on, sometimes wondering if the person was really in need, or if they were just lazy and I was an easy mark. Now, I tried to pause and exchange a few words, make eye contact, and wish them well. At first, it felt awkward and clumsy. But I still noticed a feeling of connection. For a brief moment, our lives intersected, and it felt good. Now I don't worry about whether their need is genuine or whether I am being a schmuck; I just hope in some way I am helping.

A commitment to kindness asks me to overcome barriers and sharpen skills. It asks me to engage in new ways, not just with *my* life but also with Life with a capital *L.*

It doesn't matter if I'm the only one aware of my effort to be kind. What matters is my intention. Undoubtedly, there will be times when I slip—when I speak sharply or fail to notice an opportunity to extend kindness. But each offered kindness smooths the path of our shared journey and adds another glimmer of hope to the world. Each kindness affirms Henry James's assertion that kindness is the most important gift we can offer.

Kindness in Action: *Think about how you interact with people throughout your days: Are you generally kind . . . or just nice? Try doing something kindly that you usually do nicely; can you feel a difference? Think about the messages you received as a child. Were you encouraged to share, to "extend kindness"? Or were you warned about scarcity, advised to hold on to what you have and keep trying to accumulate more? What messages serve you now, and what message would you share with the children in your life? Consider posting a simple reminder, such as "Extend Yourself," where you will see it often.*

Chapter 2:

If I Were Always Kind,
I Wouldn't Be Doing This

"When we do what we love, again and again, our life comes to hold the fragrance of that thing." (Wayne Muller)

I am not an inherently kind person. It's difficult to admit that. Kindness is the quality I value most, yet sometimes I still struggle with it. Friends and acquaintances frequently tell me that I'm kind, and I certainly wish it were true, because there's nothing I'd rather be, but kindness is often difficult. I can be snarky. I can be judgmental. I can be shy, abrupt, or oblivious. And cranky. For many years, I would say cranky was my default setting. Maybe that's why my year of living kindly mattered so much to me.

I have always admired people who are kind, and I wanted to be like them. I love how good it feels just to be around them. But wanting doesn't make it so. Several years ago, I went on a weeklong vision quest to commemorate a milestone birthday. I had no particular intention for the occasion, other than to experience something new and challenge myself physically. In fact, I deliberately set no expectations or objectives for the adventure, for once allowing whatever happened to happen without attempting to control the outcome (other than survival—that was nonnegotiable). I tend not to be a very "woo-woo" person, so I scoffed at the notion of spirit messengers and mystical experiences. I just hoped I wouldn't encounter snakes or exceptionally large spiders.

Returning from seven days in Death Valley where I fasted alone in the desert for half that time, I was proud to have faced the physical challenge I had set for myself, but I also realized that I was carrying back a new sense of purpose I hadn't actively been seeking. While kindness was already something I thought about and aspired to, my commitment had been, at best, halfhearted. I realized, though, that kindness had been my companion in the desert. As someone who had never before camped, backpacked, slept in anything but a comfortable bed—or even peed outdoors—I had experienced nothing but kindness: from the guides who prepared me for the journey; from my husband, who was completely bewildered by my desire to undertake this quest but who supported me wholeheartedly; from nature, which offered me breathtaking beauty and mild conditions (and no snakes!); and from myself in accepting my own inexperience without judgment. Writing in my journal and speaking to the quiet canyon that had been my temporary desert home, I recognized one true thing: living a kind life was what mattered most, and learning how to do that was the goal I placed in front of me from that day forward.

Wouldn't it be great if I could tell you that setting the intention was all it took? But no, I all-too-quickly resumed my cranky ways, stopping and starting kindness like a sputtering engine. Sometimes I was kind. Sometimes I even went out of my way to be kind, but often I was oblivious, irritable, lazy, or just "too busy." Our company was growing rapidly, and sixty-five to seventy-five-hour workweeks were my norm. Who had time to be kind? A few years went by; kindness was frequently in my thoughts, but I didn't make it a priority, or when I did, the mood faded when faced with anything that made it hard or inconvenient.

Was I a bitch? No, not really, not usually. I just wasn't ready to claim my kindness.

That's why I finally embarked on a year of living kindly and chose to blog about it. Putting the intention out there and inviting friends and strangers to read about it meant that if I shrugged off kindness or let it fall by the wayside, it wouldn't just be noticeable to me, but also to people who were watching my progress and supporting it. That extra visibility helped me stay focused when work deadlines or personal challenges confronted me. Best of all, I saw that kindness strengthened my resolve; it engendered more kindness, and I started to own kindness as a quality I apply in my daily life.

Huzzah for me. End of story.

No, it's not, because kindness isn't a destination, and it most certainly isn't something that one achieves and from that day forward always has at the ready. What I realized as the year progressed is that kindness is something I must commit to every morning, something I keep in my awareness, and something I recommit to when I stumble off the path (which still happens occasionally and always will). It was a joyous commitment, though; it felt like I was connecting to my truest and best self. For me, blogging was the strategy that finally held my feet to the proverbial fire, but it might just as easily have been journaling, meditating, sharing my commitment with one good friend, or connecting with nature. It also helped me to recognize that there would and will be times when I fall short. I learned finally not to let perfection get in the way of intention. Each of us will find our own pathway to maintaining our commitment to change, whether it's developing a skill, altering a habit, or adopting a new behavior. What's yours?

I suppose if I were an innately kind person, I wouldn't need to think about kindness; it would come naturally and easily. But there are still days when, as soon as words come out of my mouth, I recognize that they were not especially kind and contributed nothing of value. It's gratifying to see that the more I pay attention to kindness and to my own reactions and responses, the more I am able to be kind. What we choose to say, and to leave unsaid, conveys volumes about who we are.

Kindness in Action: Are there things in your life that you wish you had—qualities, talents, abilities, even possessions? How committed are you to acquiring them? Are there some that you think about but have little interest in striving toward? And others that you are willing to commit your energy and time to developing and achieving? We can't go after everything that we find appealing in life, but we can focus on those things that resonate most clearly and deeply for us. Knowing what matters may be one of the secrets to a satisfying life. What matters to you? If kindness is one of the things that matter to you, make a plan for committing to it every day . . . and watch how your life changes. Look for a reinforcing activity, whether it be blogging, sharing your commitment with a friend, meditating, journaling, or whatever fuels your passion.

Chapter 3:

The Chasm between Kindness and Unkindness

"Kindness. Easy to do. Easy not to do. Choose the latter, no one will notice. Choose the former and lives may change."
(Julian Bowers Brown)

I am rarely unkind. I think that's true of most of us. I can think of only a few times in recent years when I have behaved unkindly, and thinking of them makes me cringe. I may have been short-tempered with an employee, or sarcastic toward a telemarketer. I wish I could have a do-over. I'm not proud of those instances; I've learned that I never feel good about myself afterward. I hope they are rare and becoming rarer. But the fact that I am generally not unkind does not make me kind, just as the fact that I own a set of golf clubs does not make me a golfer.

As I tried to claim kindness as my own, I saw that it was one thing to be able to swallow a snarky remark if one is made in my direction, or to smile tolerantly if someone's actions inconvenience me. It was another thing entirely to let the remark pass without judgment, or to genuinely accept inconvenience with a sincere and reassuring smile and without a prickle of resentment. That, I saw, was the difference between being kind and not being unkind. They're worlds apart!

I know very few people whom I would describe as unkind, and I am blessed to know many who are extraordinarily kind. They give me hope for the world. In between, there's a vast majority of people who are neither kind nor unkind, but who reside in that ravine between the two: a chasm of ambivalence and detachment.

I was reminded of the power of kindness on a flight home from Detroit a few years back. The airline kept posting notices delaying the flight with no explanation for the reason. I watched my fellow passengers grow irritated. They fumed about incompetence; some yelled, threatened, or cursed. They bullied and berated the gate attendant—who had absolutely no control over the situation. She apologized over the loudspeaker and assured us in a calm voice that we would be informed as soon as she was given any updates. The impatient grumbling in the waiting area got louder, and people became increasingly vocal in their anger and dissatisfaction.

As a frequent flyer, I tend to be fairly resigned to delays and always have a book to distract me from the waiting. I've never seen anger or impatience improve a situation such as this. As I watched the gate attendant deal patiently and respectfully with one angry person after another, I wondered if I could display the same professionalism and politeness under similar circumstances. I rather doubted it. When there was finally a break at her desk I felt compelled to say something to her—maybe I needed to differentiate myself from the pack, or maybe I just wanted to let her know that her grace under pressure was noticed and appreciated. I walked up to the desk and simply said, "I just want to tell you that I admire how professionally you are handling this. I don't know how you are able to maintain courtesy and patience with everyone—no matter how rude they are to you. I'm sorry you have to deal with this. Thank you."

She looked at me with relief that I hadn't been another angry customer. Then she thanked me for my words and for easing the stress she was feeling. I sat down, glad that I had spoken up, and thought that was the end of that.

A few minutes later, I watched her take a call at her ticket desk. She spoke into the phone for a few moments, tapped on her computer, and then hung up. She looked up and around the waiting area. Her eyes met mine and she made a small gesture with her finger that I should come to the desk. When I got there she told me in a low voice that she had just learned that our flight had been canceled and all passengers would need to rebook. She asked me if Seattle was my final destination. I told her yes. She asked to look at my ticket, tapped on her computer for a few moments, and said, "There's an American flight leaving in twenty-five minutes from Gate 17. I've just booked you on it. I was even able to get you an aisle seat."

As my documents issued from the printer, I thanked her profusely. She smiled and pointed me in the direction of Gate 17. Walking away, I heard her announce the flight cancellation and saw the mass of passengers descend on her, each rushing to be first in line to rebook their flight.

Slipping into my aisle seat a few minutes later, I marveled at the fact that not only had my flight problem been resolved painlessly, I had received a wonderful lesson in the power of kindness. Choosing to say something kind to ease another's stress had yielded a result I hadn't anticipated and one I wouldn't have enjoyed had I joined the belligerent throng or simply remained silent. I think I smiled all the way to Seattle.

Even if I do not behave unkindly, and even if I am able someday to dispel unkind thoughts, that will not make me kind. Kindness is a lot more than not being unkind. There's that immense chasm between kind and unkind, and it's filled with all the things that get in the way of our kindness, such as:

- Fear
- Laziness
- Impatience

- Indifference
- Inertia
- Obliviousness
- Shyness
- Habit

. . . to name just a few. At one time or another, each of these may be a barrier both to being kind and to accepting kindness from others. For me, shyness is sometimes a barrier. I haven't entirely shed admonitions from childhood to "never draw attention to yourself." Extending kindness might mean treading into unfamiliar territory: *putting myself out there.* Offering help to a stranger, speaking up, stepping in . . . these aren't always second nature to me. We'll be talking about all of these—and more—in the pages to come.

If I am to spend less time in the chasm and more on the kindness side of the canyon, I'll need to climb over and out of those limiting responses. That takes awareness and action . . . and a readiness to admit when I fall short. It also takes a willingness to be vulnerable. I hope you will come to agree with me that it's well worth the climb.

Kindness in Action: Can you think of instances when you have been unkind or failed to extend kindness when an opportunity arose? Or when you thought about speaking up, but didn't? How do those recollections make you feel? Self-awareness is a key element of kindness. Can you identify limiting behaviors or beliefs that may sometimes be an obstacle to your own kindness? What's one kind thing that you can do today, or this week, to demonstrate your commitment to living a kinder life?

Chapter 4:

Kindness and Indifference

Cannot Coexist

"They say philosophers and wise men are indifferent. Wrong. Indifference is a paralysis of the soul, a premature death."
(Anton Chekhov)

While the opposite of kindness is, logically, unkindness, I think equally opposite is indifference. One cannot be kind if caring is absent. Unless we are willing to suspend our spectator status and jump into our lives, we will probably wallow in a state of relatively comfortable indifference. But indifference and kindness cannot coexist.

How many times have we seen something disturbing or inappropriate and shrugged, thinking, "It's not my problem," or "I don't want to get involved"? Sometimes it's a question of safety: *Is there some potential of danger if I step in?* Or disruption to our schedule: *I don't have time to get involved.* There's even something called compassion fatigue, where we are simply so burned out by all the craziness and tragedy we see in the media that we are numb to it when it's right in front of us.

One of the most notorious examples of indifference occurred in the 1960s in New York City. A young woman named Kitty Genovese was savagely murdered in plain sight of many—none of whom lifted a finger to help. Dozens of people were awakened by her screams and even watched from their windows as she was attacked and stabbed over a prolonged period. Yet none tried to intervene or even picked up the phone to call the police. It seems unbelievable that no one would step up to help in any way. But they didn't want to get involved; they couldn't be bothered; they were afraid; perhaps they assumed someone else had already taken action.

Indifference to a crime such as the Genovese murder appalls us all, but at a more subtle level, don't we demonstrate indifference to many other things in our lives, things we see around us every day: poverty, homelessness, inequality, injustice, bullying, and the ordinary needs of others? Too often, we wearily say, "What can I do?" Or we perfect our ability to ignore the problem; we shrug and look away. Sometimes—especially in the face of big issues with no easy solutions—it's easy to forget that every kindness has a ripple, and even if we can't solve the problem, we can alleviate the suffering or lighten the load for one person. And the action we take might inspire someone else to take a similar action and help one more person. The ripples are endless. There is no such thing as a small kindness.

We learn indifference from the people around us. Children, especially, model what they see, and from the time they are very young, they see a great deal of indifference. They may question it at first: "Why don't we stop and help?" or "How come that man doesn't have a place to live?" Soon, though, when the adults around them don't seem to care, they stop caring, too. They learn indifference. They, too, shrug and say, "Whatever."

But just as indifference is learned, so is kindness. The earlier we start learning kindness, the sooner we are able to practice it, thus staving off indifference. It's up to each of us to resist the numbing comfort of our own apathy and practice being fully engaged in our lives.

Kindness and empathy are antidotes to indifference. We cannot force kindness, any more than we can force love or respect. But the sooner we can replace shrugs with caring, and averting our eyes with a smile and a genuine response, we will be on the way to countering indifference and engaging fully in what poet Mary Oliver calls our "one wild and precious life."

***Kindness in Action:** Can you think of an instance of indifference—your own or someone else's—where a much-needed kindness was deterred? Reimagine the scenario, replacing indifference with empathy and action. Imagine, also, a future situation where you may witness injustice, cruelty, or hardship. How would you like to respond? Picture it as vividly as you can—don't be afraid to be the hero of your imaginings. Anticipating how you might respond—even down to the details of how you might stand and what you might say—prepares you to take action in a real situation should it come your way. Engagement and involvement are the hallmarks of a life well lived. When you face the choice between detachment and connection, what will you choose?*

II. Why Kindness Matters:
Its Benefits and Power

Chapter 5:

Perform Two Acts of Kindness
and Call Me in the Morning

"When you carry out acts of kindness you get a wonderful feeling inside. It is as though something inside your body responds and says, yes, this is how I ought to feel." (Harold Kushner)

Kindness really is its own reward, but if there are some bonuses that go along with it, I'm all for that. It appears that there are quite a few related to our health and well-being.

There is a growing body of evidence that kindness is not only good for the world, it's good for our physical and mental health. In fact, it may just be a wonder drug. Perhaps someday soon, instead of giving us a prescription for some unpronounceable pharmaceutical, our doctor will advise us to watch *Enchanted April* and bake some cookies for a neighbor.

Kindness Increases Happiness and Reduces Depression

In an April 2014 article entitled "The Act of Kindness and Its Positive Health Benefits"[1], Danica Collins reported that there are numerous scientific studies showing that acts of kindness have a positive effect on the body's immune system, as well as on the production of serotonin in the brain. Serotonin is a chemical created by the human body that works as a neurotransmitter, and has a calming, antianxiety effect. Scientists say that a deficiency of serotonin leads to depression.

When people perform acts of kindness, they benefit from a boost to the immune system and an increase in serotonin production. The recipient of the kind act derives the same benefits, and—most surprising of all—people who merely *witness* an act of kindness get a similar boost.

Ms. Collins goes on to report that the benefits of kindness don't stop there. She cites research that people who are routinely kind get relief from chronic pain, stress, and insomnia, and they have increases in happiness, optimism, and self-worth. Wonder drug, indeed!

Positive Side Effects

As I consciously chose kindness, I started to notice so many interesting things: I was happier, plain and simple—I felt lighter and more confident. It also seemed to me that the people around me were kinder—strangers, colleagues, acquaintances—and seemed happier and more open, too. Was I just projecting my feelings on other people, or was kindness like some sort of contagion—spread through human contact? As I did more investigation, I saw that this was exactly what was happening.

Scottish scientist David R. Hamilton, PhD, has done considerable research[2] into the health benefits of kindness. He reports that there are five beneficial "side effects" of kindness:

1. Kindness makes us happier: Dr. Hamilton notes that kindness elevates the levels of dopamine in the brain, giving us what he calls a "natural high."

2. Kindness is good for your heart: He reports that acts of kindness often generate an emotional warmth that produces the hormone oxytocin in the brain and body. This, in turn, releases nitric oxide in the blood vessels, causing them to dilate and lower one's blood pressure, which acts as a cardioprotective agent. Oxytocin also reduces levels of free radicals and inflammation in the cardiovascular system, thus reducing heart disease.

3. Kindness slows aging: That same reduction of free radicals and inflammation slows aging in the human body. Dr. Hamilton notes that compassion has similarly been linked to activity in the vagus nerve, which also regulates heart rate and controls inflammation levels in the body.

4. Kindness improves relationships: Dr. Hamilton claims that connecting with one another is actually a genetic predisposition. "Our evolutional ancestors had to learn to cooperate with one another. The stronger the emotional bonds within groups, the greater the chances of survival, so 'kindness genes' were etched into the human genome," he explains. As a result, kindness builds new relationships and boosts existing ones.

5. Kindness is contagious: Just as colds and flu are contagious in a bad way, so is kindness in a good way. "When we're kind," Hamilton says, "we inspire others to be kind, and it actually creates a ripple effect that spreads outwards to our friends' friends' friends—to three degrees of separation."

As an example of that ripple effect, Dr. Hamilton tells the story of an anonymous individual who donated a kidney to a stranger. It triggered a ripple of family members donating their kidneys to others, the domino effect ultimately spanning the breadth of the US and resulting in ten people receiving kidneys as a consequence of one anonymous donor.

Dr. Hamilton further finds that in extending kindness and compassion, we change our brains. He says that acts of kindness "find their way into the chemistry and structure of our brain. If kindness becomes a habit, we can significantly alter the wiring of our brain." He likens it to learning a new skill, such as playing a musical instrument. As we continue to practice, we bring about chemical and structural changes that establish "kindness circuits" in our brains, and we wire ourselves for more and more kindness. We replace negative habits with positive ones, selfish behaviors with kind ones, hostility with empathy, and complaints with gratitude. I'd call that a wonder drug, wouldn't you?

Best of all, there aren't multiple paragraphs of small-print warnings accompanying a dose of kindness. Kindness has never been shown to cause nausea, constipation, diarrhea, skin rashes, or drowsiness! Nor should it be avoided if you are operating heavy machinery.

Next time you perform an act of kindness, or you are the beneficiary of one—or if you simply witness a kindness—pause and notice all the good things you are feeling. Want to feel that way all the time? It's easy. You know what to do.

But Wait, There's More

In addition to the direct health benefits of kindness, there's also growing evidence that kindness and empathy in our health care practitioners have a measurable impact on our health and healing. Research is showing that a doctor's disposition and attitude toward his or her patients influences their well-being and their recovery. Researchers at the University of Wisconsin

School of Medicine reported[3] that patients whose doctors expressed empathy suffered from a cold for one day fewer than patients whose physicians focused on just the symptoms of the illness. They reported that physician empathy also boosted the patients' immune systems. There was a direct relation between a physician's empathy level and her patient's level of IL-8, a chemical that activates immune system cells to fight disease. This is just one of many recent studies confirming the importance of kindness and empathy in health care providers. *Kind doctors have better outcomes.*

Of course, focusing on a physician's kindness or empathy in no way diminishes the importance of his or her competence. The best care must involve both. David Haslam, chair of the UK's National Institute for Health and Care Excellence (NICE), has written[4] that kindness, compassion, and trust "are the pillars supporting the whole structure of care" in the British National Health Service. He notes that these important values are not optional extras in the health care system: "They are core, central, vital. . . . they have a profound effect on outcomes."

Dr. James Doty, professor of neurosurgery at the Stanford University School of Medicine, notes that "kindness, compassion, and empathy have a profound effect on healing."[5] He reports that evidence from psychology, neuroscience, and even economics supports the importance of human connection between patient and physician in improving physiology and health. Without such connection, there is evidence that "immune function and wound healing can be negatively affected."

Jeffrey Young, writing for Dignity Health[6], cites several studies that support the health benefits of compassionate care. He references a study in *Social Science & Medicine*[7] finding that patients of courteous and sympathetic doctors showed marked improvements in symptoms of irritable bowel syndrome and quality of life. He also cites a study in the *Canadian Medical Association Journal*[8] that found that kind, respectful communication between doctor and patient improves patients' emotional health and results in faster recovery. Yet another study[9] showed that a doctor's ability to empathize and listen effectively yields better pain relief outcomes.

Today, medical schools are putting more emphasis on developing the physicians' interpersonal skills and empathy, as well as their technical competence—a change from the long-standing effort to train stoic and paternalistic physicians. Knowing that burnout is a serious issue for doctors and other health care practitioners, it is my hope that kindness, compassion, and improved communication not only benefit the patient but also help the physician to better cope with the stress and pressures of their important job.

As pharmaceutical companies search for the next magic pill, we would do well to remember that kindness may be the best medicine of all!

Kindness in Action: *Next time you feel a headache coming on or feel fatigued by stress, look for the first opportunity to extend a kindness and pay attention to what that feels like. Did it reduce or eliminate the headache, or ease your stress? Along those same lines, if your partner, friend, or child is depressed or feeling poorly, see if your genuine expression of kindness can help them feel better.*

Can you think of a movie where kindness ultimately prevails that you could watch whenever you want a boost? Some of my favorites are classics such as Harvey *(1950),* Ruggles of Red Gap *(1935),* You Can't Take It with You *(1938), and* Mr. Deeds Goes to Town *(1936). Others are a bit newer:* Enchanted April *(1991),* Pride *(2014),* Charlotte's Web *(2006), and* Pay It Forward *(2000). Undoubtedly you'll have your own favorites. Parents can find an extensive list of movies that help kids recognize and understand kindness at: www.commonsensemedia.org/ lists/movies-that-inspire-compassion.*

If your physicians or health care practitioners express kindness and respond empathetically to you, take time to thank them for both the professional and emotional care they provide you.

Chapter 6:

Bibbidi-Bobbidi-Boo: Kindness Alleviates Social Anxiety

"If you want others to be happy, practice compassion. If you want to be happy, practice compassion." (Dalai Lama)

Imagine if Cinderella had been too shy to go to the ball. It would have been a very different story, or no story at all. Had she demurred when her fairy godmother offered her a shimmering gown, glass slippers, and a golden coach, her fate would have been to continue as servant and drudge to her demanding stepmother and selfish stepsisters. Years later, tired and worn down by life, she might have thought regretfully about the night she said no because she was too afraid to say yes. So much for happily ever after.

Fortunately for her—and for six-year-old girls everywhere—Cindy was confident and eager to suit up and ride her pimped-out pumpkin to the palace where she became the belle of the ball.

But there are thousands of people who face Cindy's choice daily—though on a smaller and less Disneyesque scale—and they hold back, out of fear and social anxiety. They feel a paralyzing dread at the thought of entering a social situation—be it attending a party, meeting new people, or speaking out in a classroom or at a meeting. Help is at hand, though, in the form of new research showing that *kindness alleviates social anxiety.*

Social anxiety is more than shyness. According to the Social Anxiety Institute, "Social anxiety is the fear of interaction with other people that brings on self-consciousness, feelings of being negatively judged and evaluated, and, as a result, leads to avoidance . . . feelings of inadequacy, inferiority, embarrassment, humiliation, and depression."[1] It is a debilitating condition, isolating the sufferers and often preventing them from developing intimacy or close relationships.

A study[2] by researchers Jennifer Trew of Simon Fraser University and Lynn Alden of the University of British Columbia revealed that engaging in acts of kindness reduced levels of social anxiety and social avoidance.

The study divided college students with social anxiety issues into three groups. One was directed to simply keep a diary of their experiences and emotions, another was exposed to different socialization situations, and the third was instructed to perform acts of kindness—three acts of kindness a day for two days a week over the course of four weeks. The kindnesses could be as simple as shoveling the snow on a neighbor's walk, donating to charity, or cleaning up after a roommate, and were defined as "acts that benefit others or make others happy, typically at some cost to oneself."

After a month, the group tasked with performing acts of kindness reported lower levels of discomfort and anxiety about social interaction than either of the other two groups.

The researchers concluded that "acts of kindness may help to counter negative social expectations by promoting more positive perceptions (and expectations) of the social environment. This is likely to occur early in the intervention as participants anticipate positive reactions from others in response to their kindness, decreasing the perceived need to avoid negative social outcomes."

So . . . we feel better about ourselves and our environment when we extend kindness, and we also expect better reactions and results. Thus, we are less fearful. It's an upward spiral.

I suspect, also, that when we are engaged in kind acts, our attention is on the act or the object of it, and we are less aware of our own worries. While this study didn't specifically look at people performing kindnesses in the social situations that frighten them, I imagine entering such situations with the intent of finding opportunities to be kind would go far to alleviate the fear. It would divert us from feeling self-conscious and worrying about how we are being judged. It may be as simple as befriending someone who is sitting alone at a meeting or conference—focusing on alleviating another person's discomfort will lessen your own.

While most of us don't suffer from debilitating social anxiety, this study of kindness can likely be generalized to anyone who experiences discomfort in social situations—whether a cocktail party, public speaking event, wedding, funeral, or the dating scene.

Throughout many years of working with associations and nonprofits, the things I dreaded most were the ubiquitous cocktail parties and conference receptions. I think people either love or hate these events. As an introvert, I lean toward the latter. I do fine one-on-one or in groups where there is a solid reason for the meeting, but the idea of just walking up to strangers and engaging in small talk or inserting myself into clusters of people already in conversation made my stomach churn. I would put in an appearance at these events and escape as soon as possible. But as I committed to kindness, I tried to change the lens through which I view the dreaded cocktail party. There must be plenty of other people like me who are uncomfortable at these functions. Maybe instead of focusing on myself, I could look for others who may be standing uncomfortably alone and see if I could help them. So I did that. I even signed up to chair the event in one organization I belong to—it gave me the perfect way to introduce myself and open the conversation. I asked people how they were enjoying the conference, if there was anything in particular they hoped to get out of it, if there were any people they especially wanted to meet. If there were and I knew those people—or knew someone who might—I would try to initiate that introduction.

Wow! What a difference it made to turn my attention from my own discomfort to someone else's comfort. I found I was staying through entire events—and enjoying myself. Plus, throughout the remainder of the conference, I had more people to network and talk with—many of whom became friends and close business colleagues.

My experience supported the research on social anxiety. If we replace worrying with looking for opportunities to be kind, we may very well discover that the event we dreaded was enjoyable and painless. And perhaps we'll be the proverbial belle of the ball.

As Cinderella might say, "If the shoe fits . . ."

Kindness in Action: *If you sometimes suffer from social anxiety, think of how you could put some of these suggestions into practice. Could you extend small kindnesses proactively to alleviate future discomforts? Could you go to that dreaded wedding reception or cocktail party with the intention of focusing on others and behaving compassionately rather than dwelling on your own uneasiness? And if social anxiety isn't a problem for you, think about how you could ease someone else's apprehension at a business meeting or social event.*

Chapter 7:

An Epidemic of Our Own Choosing

"Let us learn to live with kindness, to love everyone, even when they do not love us." (Pope Francis)

Every time there is a major election on the horizon, I hope that will be the year when candidates engage in civil discourse and voters are able to choose from among an array of thoughtful, wise, and courteous public servants. Those hopes are usually dashed before the first debate. To my horror, candidates engage in incivility that would cause them to have their mouths rinsed out with soap, or at least an extended time-out, if they were really the eight-year-olds they act like.

But they are adult men and women, and for many of them, name-calling, lying, and rudeness are standard operating procedures. And, sadly, their supporters cheer and egg them on, giving tacit approval for boorish behavior. I fear that, as some assert, we get the politicians we deserve.

It's not just elections—though they are certainly one of the most prominent examples. We see it in sports rivalries, or when something in the news raises a double-edged fervor. Rude and boorish behavior descends on us like an epidemic. And, sadly, that's what it is.

According to a study[1] by researchers at the University of Florida, *rudeness is contagious*. Really, it spreads like a cold or the flu—it's passed from one person to the next until most everybody's got it. Not only do people who are subjected to rude treatment themselves subsequently behave rudely, even those who only witness rudeness succumb to rude behaviors.

The study asserts that, "Just like the common cold, common negative behaviors can spread easily." Lead researcher Trevor Foulk further stated[2], "It's very easy to catch. Just a single incident, even observing a single incident, can cause you to be more rude. . . . Rudeness is contagious, when I experience it, I become rude."

"Part of the problem," he added, "is that we are generally tolerant of these behaviors, but they're actually really harmful." Where outright abuse and aggression are far more infrequent—and less readily accepted—rudeness is something people face daily, and its effects can be devastating.

"Rudeness is largely tolerated," Foulk said. "We experience rudeness all the time in organizations because organizations allow it."

Maybe our political candidates and certain media personalities should come with a warning label: *Caution: listening to this person could be hazardous to your humanity.*

Perhaps most concerning is the study's revelation that all of this happens at an unconscious level. "What we found in this study," said Foulk, "is that the contagious effect is based on an automatic cognitive mechanism—automatic means it happens somewhere in the subconscious part of your brain, so you don't know it's happening and can't do much to stop it."

Does that mean that those people who abhor what a particular politician or commentator says and stands for, but who may watch him for entertainment or in morbid disbelief, are nonetheless "catching" his rudeness? Sounds like it.

Responding to the study[3], Barbara Mitchell, human

resources consultant and author of *The Essential Workplace Conflict Handbook,* says rude behavior can be stopped if it's clear to all that such behavior will not be tolerated. "To me it starts from the top. . . . How does the leadership behave? What kind of culture do they want? And how do they live their own values within the organization?" She further notes that bad behavior must be addressed immediately. It must be made clear to everyone the moment it surfaces that rudeness will not be tolerated.

While she is talking about workplace incivility, it stands to reason that the same factors exist at a broader, cultural level. How do our leaders behave? What values do they model? What are we—as members of that culture—willing to tolerate? And how about in social media? Are we tolerating—or even propagating—offensive behaviors that spread to all corners of cyberspace? It also holds true at a micro level. If incivility is acceptable in family discourse, the members of the family are more likely to be rude and indifferent both inside and outside the family.

If being treated rudely, or even just witnessing rude treatment, causes people to behave more rudely themselves, is it any wonder that we tend to see an escalation of discourtesy as elections progress and as sporting championships are decided? Where will it end?

If we want to advance a kind and courteous culture, we need to take a stand. We need to politely say "no" when a politician speaks disrespectfully of an opponent, a dissenter, or a group of people—or when the media or political pundits engage in name-calling or deceit. We need to let people know it's not okay to be disrespectful in any setting. We need to say, "That's not acceptable," and turn our backs if they persist. That's how the contagion is countered.

Fortunately, It Works Both Ways

The news isn't all bad. We talked about this in Chapter 5, but it bears repeating: there's also ample research that kindness can spread like a contagion, too. Scottish scientist David Hamilton,

PhD, who has extensively researched the health benefits of kindness, claims that kindness is just as contagious—in a good way—as colds, flu, and rudeness are in a bad way. He describes the ripple effect of kind actions, spreading outward to three degrees of separation—to our friends' friends' friends. And just as rudeness contaminates the perpetrator, the recipient, and witnesses, so does kindness infect the giver, the receiver, and witnesses. Whether one extends kindness, receives kindness, or merely witnesses kindness, the result is the same: it acts as a catalyst for more kindness.

So it appears that we can choose what sorts of bugs we will expose ourselves to, and whether we want to be an instigator for rudeness or for kindness. We can choose whether we want to breathe the air of reckless incivility or of well-mannered courtesy. Each time we choose, we reinforce our support for the world as we want it to be. Isn't it time for an epidemic of kindness? It's within our power.

Kindness in Action: *Think about whether the "entertainment value" of watching people behave badly (in the media, on reality TV, or in our day-to-day encounters) is worth the risks of exposure. When you see or experience such behaviors, how can you counter them without absorbing them yourself? Try responding with kindness to see if you can turn a negative contagion into a positive one. Remember that you always have a choice regarding what behaviors you will tolerate and—especially—how you will respond. Your kindness can turn the tide.*

Chapter 8:

The Business Case for Kindness

"We live under the illusion that organizations are 'them' when, in reality, they are 'us.' If we wish to work in evolved organizations, we must each be the first to start the journey."
(Lance Secretan)

Several years ago, one of our company's longtime employees retired. At her retirement party, she said that, if asked, the word she would use to describe the company was "kind." I remember thinking at the time that I could think of no word I would rather hear used to describe our business.

Oh, sure, I wanted us to be daringly *innovative* and wildly *profitable*, but even above these qualities, I wanted us to be kind. Since that day when Margaret labeled our company's defining trait, I think we were more conscious of that value and more committed to it. That's not to say we didn't slip occasionally. We're human, after all, and the business world can certainly challenge the kindest intentions.

It isn't easy to always be kind in business, and there may be times when kindness is well-disguised, but if the underlying culture is kind, the intention generally shines through. Whether we were interviewing, training, correcting, or even terminating an employee, we did our utmost to approach it kindly—using empathy and compassion. In client or vendor situations, likewise, when problems arose we looked for solutions that were fair and respectful to all. We also looked for clients who shared our values. Clients who practiced kindness themselves. Clients who didn't put the blame on others for mistakes they made, and didn't ask us to bend our integrity on their behalf.

A few years ago, after managing a large conference, a couple of our staff noticed that the hotel had missed a sizable food and beverage charge on the bill. The client's convention chair directed them to pay the bill quickly and not point out the error. Our staff followed their consciences rather than his instructions. They pointed out the error to the hotel and asked for a corrected bill. The chairman was not happy, but we were honest with the board of directors and other organizational leaders and told them integrity came first. They agreed, and I believe it solidified our relationship—we both understood that we could trust one another to do the right thing.

In doing this, our team not only did the right thing, but also modeled our values to our client and to their office colleagues. The longer I am in business, the more certain I am that success lies in working with people—employees, clients, suppliers, business partners—who share our values. Over the years, we have made the decision to sever our relationships with a few clients, usually because of a troubling difference in our values, or because of how we saw them treating our employees or others with whom they interacted. We never once regretted our decision, though often we regretted that we hadn't made it sooner.

I can still vividly remember my first real "nine-to-five" job after college. It was for a publishing company that was a holding of a large, publically traded corporation. The president of our relatively small division was a bully. He motivated—if that's what you call it—by fear and intimidation. That was about the time that a variety of books on *winning through intimidation, looking out for number one,* and *nice guys finish last* were gaining in popularity. I'm pretty sure our company president stayed up nights studying these texts and planning how he was going to terrorize and coerce the editorial and sales teams working under him. It was a "profit at any price" era, a time when the word "cutthroat" held positive connotations. At that time, many business leaders would have scoffed at the notion of a kind workplace.

"Kindness has no place in business," they would have said. "It's soft, it's weak, it's squishy."

Today, we're learning that just the opposite is true. Treating people with kindness and encouragement brings out their best work. The carrot really is far more effective than the stick. Writing for *Forbes*, David K. Williams[1] reports on organizational psychology research from the Queens School of Business and the Gallup Organization showing that "a negative, cutthroat environment leads employees to become disengaged. And a business with a disengaged workforce will experience, on average, 16 percent lower profitability and a 65 percent lower share price over time than a business with an engaged workforce." Today, three-quarters of the US workforce is said to be disengaged. An alarming statistic!

Further, Williams cites research finding that employees of companies that are generally described as having kind cultures have 20 percent higher performance and are 87 percent less likely to leave. These factors, he notes, "make a big difference to the bottom line." Every business owner or manager knows the tolls on a business from high turnover: the financial costs, the decline in morale, the loss of productivity. What they often don't know or understand is that kindness is the antidote to these threats.

Williams further explains that kind business owners are not weak or ineffectual. They "can be just as shrewd and forceful and hard-hitting as their ruthless, scheming counterparts." They do it, he says, "by rising above and showing compassion."

The old notion that you need to be a jerk to succeed has been replaced by ever-growing evidence that the most successful leaders and businesses foster a culture of kindness, forgiveness, trust, respect, and inspiration.

The office I worked in all those years ago was three thousand miles away from the home office, yet my immediate boss trembled at the mere mention of the president's name, and a phone call from the executive office always triggered panic. The twice-yearly meetings that brought together staff from all the divisions' offices were an opportunity for him to browbeat his employees one-on-one or in small groups. He would berate, belittle, and threaten employees in front of their peers. After a national meeting, there was always a spate of resignations—mine was finally one of those. And yet he bemoaned the company's high turnover.

I worked with some really good people at that company, and I was sorry to be leaving them when I resigned. But I wasn't sorry to leave the company, its chief executive, or the pervasive culture of fear and intimidation.

I don't regret the three years I worked there. I learned a great deal, met a lot of tremendous people, traveled extensively, and developed some professional confidence. I also had an opportunity at a very early stage of my career to make some decisions about what I would and would not tolerate in my professional life. I vowed to myself that I would not work for another bully, and that I would not be a part of a culture that didn't value its employees or that relied on threats and intimidation rather than encouragement and support. I don't think I articulated it at the time, but from that day forward, I sought kind employers and managers, and when it was my turn to step into the employer/manager role, I sought to be kind and encouraging. I don't know that I always succeeded, but it was my intent.

A good leader empowers and supports her people. She recognizes that success depends on strengthening others and helping them feel good about themselves, their jobs, and the people they work with. This leads to high morale, company loyalty, and—as research is now showing—improved productivity and increased profitability.

Psychologist Emma Seppälä has reported on the costs to

organizations of having stressful or unkind cultures[2]. Those costs include higher turnover, employee disengagement, and more frequent absences. On the other hand, Seppälä's research has shown that positive and compassionate organizational cultures yield better customer service, higher productivity, greater employee engagement and commitment (and thus retention), healthier employees, and an improved bottom line.

This is not to say that there will never be a need for criticism, correction, or discipline, but when applied firmly, fairly, and with compassion, the results are positive and constructive. Feedback isn't always going to be positive—we'd never learn or improve if it was. But any manager or leader who thinks a steady stream of negative feedback will motivate employees and make them eager to improve is woefully misguided. And the research shows that employees who receive kind correction, or who even witness compassionate correction of other employees, perform better and experience increased loyalty to their employer.

Professors Kim Cameron and Lynn Wooten of the Ross School of Business at the University of Michigan assert[3] that both positive and negative feedback are essential, but that effective motivation requires a ratio tipped heavily to the positive. They report that high-performance teams demonstrate a positive statement ratio of about 6 to 1, while low-performance teams exhibit a positive to negative ratio of 0.36 to 1.

I can't help wondering what would happen—not just in business, but in every aspect of our lives—if each of us committed to a personal goal of making six positive comments for every one negative remark. That would make for either a very positive world . . . or a very quiet one. Either way, it's an improvement.

Kindness in Action: *Think about the places you've worked, or perhaps where you would like to work. Were kindness and respect values that were not only stated, but also consistently followed? Have you ever been in a work situation where you or others were treated poorly, demeaned, or given little support? How did that feel? Think about the*

professional (and personal) values that you would like to claim, and also the boundaries you will establish for how you expect to be treated and how you will treat others. Values are decisions we make in advance . . . make sure you know what yours are. If kindness has not been a consistent and pervasive element of your organization's culture, initiate an organization-wide conversation about kindness. As a group, identify what a kind workplace looks like—and what it doesn't look like. Talk about the benefits and come up with a shared vision for evolving to and being part of a workplace where kindness is more than a pleasing buzzword.

For the next two weeks—in both your business and personal life—try applying the six-to-one ratio: six positive comments to every one negative comment you make. Is that easy for you, or do you have to bite back snarky comments and ferret around for positive ones? After two weeks, try it for another two weeks.

III. Opening Stategies for a Kind Life

Chapter 9:

The Power of the Pause

"Human freedom involves our capacity to pause, to choose the one response toward which we wish to throw our weight."
(Rollo May)

Some time ago, a friend happened to be looking at the huge collection of quotations I have tacked to a bulletin board covering one wall of my den. Inexplicably, she started to cry. Then she grabbed a pen from her purse and copied down this quotation from author and Holocaust survivor Viktor Frankl:

"Between stimulus and response, there is a space. In that space is our power to choose our response. In our response lies our growth and our freedom."

"That's it exactly," she explained. "Whenever I'm tempted to take a drink, I need to pause in that space between stimulus and response. If I stop and think about it, I won't drink. If I don't, I slip and have a drink." I knew my friend was in AA and that sobriety was still a struggle for her.

I thought about Frankl's words and saw how many things they applied to. Not just alcohol, but overeating, smoking, spending . . . or any number of actions we take automatically with little or no thought. We allow an addiction or a learned response to overtake our free will. And, as Frankl describes, each time we *don't* give in to the reflex response, we grow and claim our own precious freedom a little more.

His wise words are just as relevant to kindness. Approaching the post office not long ago, I saw a man blast his horn at a woman whose car was blocking his exit. When she didn't move quickly, he blasted it again, and then a third time, even louder and longer.

Admittedly, some people are just bozos, and they always will be. But I'd like to think that if he had paused, perhaps he would have chosen a different response. Maybe he would have shrugged and looked at his watch and said, "I've got time." Or maybe he would have tried for a quick tap on the horn to alert her to his car, instead of three sharp and aggressive blasts.

I know I've been guilty of speaking sharply in response to someone else's rudeness or bad behavior. But that's *their* behavior. It becomes mine if I let their rudeness provoke me to similar conduct. I don't have to do that. I have a choice. When I react in kind, it doesn't improve the situation, and it doesn't make me feel any better.

I also know that when I snap back at someone (as often as not, my spouse), it's because I'm tired, feeling overwhelmed, inadequate, or—I admit it—hungry. A timely pause can prevent me from saying or doing something I'll later regret. It maintains harmony. A timely pause enables me to adjust my course and be the person I want to be. It's one of those lessons we learn and relearn over and over, until finally the pause becomes the automatic response.

There's a reason why our mothers used to tell us to stop and count to ten when we got angry. It's the power of the pause. There are things that need to be said and things that don't need to be said. If we pause to think before we speak, we generally know the difference.

Rotarians have the right idea. Rotary International—the service organization focused on human rights around the world—has a four-question test that helps members decide whether and how to act or speak. Before responding, they consider:

- Is it the truth?
- Is it fair to all concerned?
- Will it build goodwill and friendship?
- Will it be beneficial to all concerned?

If the answer to any of these questions is no, they keep silent. Wise people, those Rotarians. Politicians could learn a lot from them.

There is enormous power in something as simple as a pause. It allows us to delay long enough to decide if the action we're contemplating will really get the result we want. Sometimes, when we hit pause, we recognize that we should make that pause permanent and simply do nothing, say nothing. The pause gives us the gift of grace.

There is another time when the pause is a gift we offer ourselves—a gift of appreciation. Next time you perform an act of kindness, or you are the beneficiary of one, or you simply witness a kindness, pause and notice all the good things you are feeling. A pause allows us to acknowledge the importance of kindness in our lives, and to reaffirm the choice we have made to walk the path of kindness.

I would put the power of the pause up against the power of the Hoover Dam. It's that big. A pause may give way to understanding; it may silence hurtful words; it may avert a broken heart. Instead of speaking or acting in instant response, taking the time to pause and think about what I want my response to activate—and why—has been transformative. In the space of that brief pause, I might totally change my reaction, or perhaps decide not to respond at all. That pause has *always* guided me to a better place.

A pause is not a vacant space. It's a place of enormous potential and growth. It's where we choose who we will be in this moment, and the next.

Kindness in Action: *Can you recall a situation where pausing before responding might have brought about a better outcome? Are there particular times when you know you are most likely to respond sharply or unkindly—such as when you are tired or frightened? Would a well-timed pause be welcome here? Set an intention to pause next time your buttons are pushed. And next time you experience or witness a kindness, pause to notice how it makes you feel.*

Chapter 10:

Kindness Means Suspending Judgment

"Be kind. Everyone you meet is carrying a heavy burden."
(Ian MacLaren)

When I am unkind, it is probably more in thought than in deed. I exercise unkind *thoughts* more often than unkind *actions*. For me, unkind thoughts seem to creep in when I am in the most ordinary of circumstances, surrounded by others who—like me—are just trying to get in, get out, and get on to the next thing.

So, what's the big deal? My thoughts are my own. Who am I harming by judging people in my head, or coming up with a few choice words to describe someone's seemingly inconsiderate behavior? If no one else, I'm wounding myself: I'm reinforcing a habit of negativity. I'm separating myself from others who may be doing the best they can under circumstances I can never know. I'm not being my best self. Where my patience and understanding might improve an encounter, instead I silently criticize. Our thoughts matter.

The grocery store my husband and I frequent is often crowded. It has narrow aisles and, occasionally, prolonged waits in the checkout line. More than once I have turned the corner of an aisle to find a shopper on his cell phone, standing in the middle of the aisle, oblivious to the fact that his cart is turned sideways and blocking not just our access to the dill pickles, but another customer trying to come from the other direction.

"Excuse me," I say, but he doesn't hear me. So I straighten his cart to clear a path. He glares at me and continues his conversation. *I get judgy.* How can people be so inconsiderate? But maybe he's not inconsiderate. Maybe he's oblivious (a little better . . . we've all been *there*). Maybe he's preoccupied by a family emergency (perhaps that's the reason for needing to make/take a phone call at the market). Give him the benefit of the doubt.

We're in line to check out behind a woman with a full cart. She watches as the checker scans and packs several bags of groceries. When all has been rung up and the checker pronounces the total, she digs into her purse and produces her coupons. Fine, we use coupons, too, although we try to have them at hand. The checker scans the coupons and announces the new total. It is only then that the woman burrows again into her cavernous handbag for her checkbook and begins writing a check. My husband and I look at each other and roll our eyes. *I get judgy.* Really, couldn't she have been writing that check while her groceries were being rung up, so all she'd need to do is fill in an amount? How inconsiderate.

I need to be better at letting go of my own righteousness and giving people the benefit of the doubt. So, she delayed us by ninety seconds, is that really worth stewing about? No, it's not. Am I able to let the annoying behavior go and see something admirable in her? Maybe she made eye contact with the checker, or said something nice; maybe she is bringing some of those groceries to a neighbor who can't get out to the store. Maybe . . .

Or maybe both of these individuals *are* selfish and self-absorbed, and there's no redeeming justification for their behavior.

Am I made better by judging them? I suppose I have the satisfaction of being right, but I've come to learn that there's a greater satisfaction in being kind.

My car is another place where it's easy to think unkind thoughts. When I see some yahoo weaving between traffic lanes at top speed, or when I follow a Corolla going twenty-five miles an hour all the way up the highway entrance and braking before merging onto the uncrowded freeway, I have unkind thoughts. *I get judgy.* I'm not a person who curses or calls the drivers foul names. I tend to call offending male drivers "sport," and females "lady," as in, "What's your hurry, lady?" or "C'mon, sport, surely your car has a second gear." Compared with the drivers who blast their horns or gesture vulgarly, I'm doing tolerably well, but certainly nothing to be proud of. I usually allow other cars to merge or to change into my lane in front of me. And I always wave and mouth "thank you" when other drivers do the same for me, but all in all, driving is—at best—a pretty neutral experience.

Suspending judgment is hard, but it's one of the first big steps in behaving kindly. A story[1] the late author Stephen Covey told illustrates how sometimes our judgments can be way off-base, and if we knew what was behind a behavior, we might think very differently. Covey was on the subway with a man whose unruly children were disrupting all the other passengers—they were running back and forth, shouting, and throwing things. Finally, Covey could take it no longer. Irritated, he told the man his children were disturbing people and asked him to control them.

The man responded with an apology and explanation: "We just came from the hospital where their mother died about an hour ago. I don't know what to think, and I guess they don't know how to handle it either."

Of course, that knowledge changed everything, and Covey's anger and irritation vanished immediately, replaced by sympathy and concern.

Sometimes the annoyances in our lives are real—the result of inconsiderate people, boorish behavior, fellow humans who think themselves superior and somehow entitled. And sometimes there may be reasons behind the annoyances that bring understanding and erase irritation. When we don't have knowledge, we tend to choose the explanation that supports our annoyance—it probably confers on us a sense of superiority. What might happen, though, if we offer the benefit of the doubt in place of harsh judgment? Even if we are wrong, haven't we chosen peace over discord, compassion over condemnation?

If I were having a bad day and spoke or acted inappropriately, I would wish that others could suspend judgment and assume that I'm not usually such a horse's ass. Kindness is offering that same acceptance to others.

Judgment is a hard habit to break, but breaking it creates a lot of space in our lives for joy and for peace. Each time we find ourselves judging someone for their behavior, their appearance, or their words, let's try asking, "Is this really useful? Does this bring me peace?"—and choose to act accordingly.

Kindness in Action: *Think about where your own unkind thoughts crop up. Is it on the road, in the supermarket, around your family, or when you're in new and potentially threatening situations? When do you become most judgy? Next time you're in one of those situations, or with a group of people, try paying attention to the judgments you make— don't judge yourself for making them, just observe and ask yourself if most of your judgments are kind or harsh. Do they feel good and bring you satisfaction? If not, try letting them go. Practice acknowledging judgment and saying to it, "No, thanks, I don't need that, you can go." It takes practice, but you can become master of the judge within.*

Chapter 11:

Kindness and Keeping Score

"Kindness is an inner desire that makes us want to do good things even if we do not get anything in return. It is the joy of our life to do them. When we do good things from this inner desire, there is kindness in everything we think, say, want, and do." (Emanuel Swedenborg)

Want to know the fastest way to drain all the joy from your relationships? And from birthdays and holidays? Make sure to keep score every chance you get. Keep track of who you give presents to and whether these people give to you in return. If they do, assess whether they spent more on their gift or you did. Track who's putting more effort or time into the relationship. Who called last, who picked up the tab for coffee, who emptied the dishwasher, who initiated romance . . . ? Always be aware of who's ahead and who's behind in the giving game. There's no better way to assure that agitation replaces peace of mind.

Seated around a luncheon table at a business meeting, I tuned into a conversation among my tablemates. A woman whom I knew only slightly was describing with unconcealed pride the electronic filing system she had created some years before to track Christmas cards.

She boasted of an elaborate program that maintained both a database of names and addresses, and a spreadsheet. "Everyone on my Christmas card list is in there, and when I get cards, I note in my spreadsheet having received them. I can even indicate whether they merely signed the card, whether it was a holiday letter, or whether they included a personal note. After the holidays, I review the list and remove anyone who didn't send a card, so next year they won't get one from me."

I remember thinking at the time that this put my own slightly obsessive-compulsive tendencies into manageable perspective. I also remember thinking I was glad I was nothing more than a nodding acquaintance with this woman—I didn't like the notion of being tracked on her spreadsheet. Actually, since I don't send Christmas cards, I wouldn't ever have made the cut to begin with. But, still, I'm not sure a friendship with this woman would have been very enjoyable.

I've thought about that conversation occasionally and realized what I am most uncomfortable with is the notion of keeping score.

Anyone who follows sports knows keeping score is essential. Athletes don't get paid many millions of dollars for romping aimlessly around on the field with other millionaires. They get paid for competing fiercely, and they get paid more for winning.

Likewise, Scrabble probably isn't as enjoyable if we agree before playing that we're not going to keep score. It's good to have a goal, and healthy competition can make a game more fun.

But relationships are not competitions—nobody wins unless everybody wins.

At the heart of kindness is the idea that we act kindly, not for any reward, but for the joy it gives us, and out of the knowledge that it is the expression of our highest and best self. If we withhold our kindness until someone proves worthy, or until they meet some standard we have arbitrarily set, aren't we being less than our finest self?

I suppose we all keep score to some degree. In a couple, one partner may wash the dishes while the other does the laundry. In a friendship, we each do what we are best able to do and hope it all balances out. The danger comes when one or both of the parties set up that spreadsheet in their head (or worse, on their computer!).

Nobody wants to be taken advantage of, and friendship is supposed to be a two-way street, but relationships are complex things. They can't be broken down into "I called him last; it's his turn to call me," or "We entertained at our house last time; it's their turn to have us over." We never know what's going on in other people's lives that may make it difficult for them to reciprocate. They may be dealing with illness, financial woes, or family issues that we are entirely unaware of. As with so many things, a kind interpretation invites us to give the benefit of the doubt.

If a relationship is so one-sided that one party does all the giving and the other does all the taking, it's absolutely reasonable to ask if this really is a relationship, and if it brings joy or satisfaction. And it's absolutely okay to decide this is no longer working and sever the connection. Being kind doesn't mean one is a pushover or an easy target. Kindness and generosity are strengths, not weaknesses.

Has keeping score ever really made anyone feel better? As soon as we start keeping score in our relationships, joy vanishes. Friendships become obligations; we're always checking to see who's ahead or whose turn it is to pick up the tab.

When we do something for someone, that should be enough. We give without expectation of receiving something in return, no strings attached. We need to let go of the internal ledger on which we record "That's one for me, zero for her."

I'm finding as I get older, I'm drawn to lightening my load—getting rid of the stuff that crowds my life. I want to lighten the load I carry in my head, too: let go of thoughts that don't bring joy, let go of tallies and ledgers and concerns about whose turn it is. Magically, that also frees my head of resentment, grudges, and disappointment.

If we're accustomed to keeping score in our relationships—whether it's with our spouse, close friends, work colleagues, or those marginal people on our Christmas card list—how do we alter that habit of mentally reckoning every interaction we have? Like any habit, it's probably hard to break, but I've seen that if we keep our eyes on the real prize—peace of mind, happiness, and the joy that comes with kindness—we'll gradually do less scorekeeping and find that we're spending more time counting our blessings.

Kindness in Action: *Where do you keep score in your life? Would you be happier if you let go of the tallying and reckoning and simply assume everyone is doing their best? Think about whether you're carrying a lot of old (or new) resentments or grudges in your head, and whether you'd feel better and lighter if you could let them go. Is it more important to you to have peace of mind or to have perfect equity in all your relationships? You can't always have both.*

Chapter 12:

"~~Kill~~ Transform 'em with Kindness": A Lesson from My Mother

"Kindness is in our power, even when fondness is not."
(Samuel Johnson)

As I mentioned earlier, I learned to be nice from my mother. She was cautious in her relationships and always ready with an out if anyone asked her to get too involved—whether it was Girl Scouts, cupcake day at school, or driving the carpool. She did her part as the mother of two in a small, suburban community, but rarely volunteered to do more. Still, she was nearly always nice.

She was not particularly kind, though, and on a few occasions I saw Mom behave in startlingly unkind ways if someone asked too much of her or pried too closely into her life. She could shut them down with a word or a look, or simply turn away. Thinking back on her now, I believe it was more important for Mom to keep distance between herself and others than to connect at any deep or meaningful level. It was safer. To some degree, her daughters inherited a similar wariness. With this knowledge, I've tried to shed some of that caution and move from *nice* to *kind*.

When I was in high school, Mom worked as a receptionist and scheduler in a large medical practice. She told me once that when people were rude or impatient toward her, she made it her goal to turn them around by "killing them with kindness." She would answer a scowl with her brightest smile, a hostile comment with sympathetic and serene understanding. She would look for ways to help—whether a glass of water, a compliment, or generous use of their name. She told me that when these people left, they often made it a point to stop by her desk and thank her for her kindness. Sometimes they even apologized for being short with her.

I remember thinking that what she was telling me was out of character with the mother I thought I knew so well. Had I ever seen her go out of her way to be friendly and helpful? I asked her if it wasn't hard to be nice to people who were so unpleasant to her.

She told me, "No, I look at it as a game. I win if I can remain nice in the face of their rudeness. And I win even more if I can influence them to change their behavior." I was not entirely comfortable with the sincerity of Mom's effort, since viewing it as a "game" seemed to put it on a par with the crosswords and word searches she enjoyed daily with her morning coffee. Still, the result was kindness, and that must count for something. Perhaps counterfeit kindness would someday lead to genuine kindness.

For some reason, her words came back to me when a few of my company colleagues and I were staffing a large four-day conference for one of our association clients. On the second day, one of our team came to me and asked if I could help them deal with a woman who had been giving them nothing but grief from the moment she had registered the day before. She complained about the parking at the hotel, the cost of the conference, the complexity of the conference brochure, and even the distance to the restrooms. She was upset now because there were two breakout sessions that she really wanted to attend, but they were scheduled at the same time, so she could attend only one.

As I walked up to her, I remembered my mother's strategy and thought I'd give it a try. After I introduced myself and asked how I could help, she declared that the conference was a huge disappointment and had obviously not been planned well. She wanted to attend two sessions that were being offered at the same time. Why, she asked, weren't we repeating sessions, so she could go to both? Or, failing that, why didn't we tape all the sessions so she could get a recording of the one she couldn't attend?

I did my best to empathize with her frustration and explain why neither of her ideas—while entirely reasonable—had been practical for this conference. Mostly I listened and absorbed her dissatisfaction. When she finally headed off to attend the session, I breathed a sigh of relief, but didn't especially feel that I had accomplished what I set out to do. I may have ameliorated her anger a bit, but that wasn't enough. I wanted to do more than just counter her negativity; I wanted to help her. My kindness felt a bit counterfeit, and incomplete—what more could I do?

As it happened, the session she was unable to attend was on a topic I had some understanding of and interest in. I checked with the team to see if they could do without me for an hour and proceeded to the room where the class was being held. I picked up two sets of the handouts and sat down to listen.

When it was over, I headed out to look for the woman our staff and some of the volunteers had dubbed "Nasty Nancy."

I found her sitting by herself in a chair by a window and asked if I could join her. She nodded curtly. I then gave her the handouts from the session she had missed and told her I had attended it and would be glad to share with her what I thought were the key points. Her eyes widened, and after a long pause she eagerly accepted. I pulled out the notes I had taken and started sharing some of the speaker's concepts that had struck me. She pulled out a pen and started making notes. Then she asked—almost shyly—if I would be willing to share my notes with her. I looked at my messy notes and then at her. "If you can read my handwriting, you're welcome to them. I'll get a copy made and have it for you at the registration desk after lunch."

She thanked me—not profusely, but genuinely—and asked me more questions about the session I had attended. *Mission accomplished*, I thought to myself.

For the remainder of the conference, there were no more complaints about "Nasty Nancy." She sought me out a few times, and once, after she had joined me at a lunch table, she admitted that she had never been to a conference this large before, and she was a bit overwhelmed by the crowds and the choices. I remembered the first big convention I had attended and identified with her anxiety. Once I saw Nancy's behavior as a response to her fear, I saw her in a new light.

I wonder if we would all be kinder if everyone walked around with thought balloons above our heads describing our circumstances: "I'm scared." "Just broke up with my girlfriend." "Haven't a clue what to do next." "I don't want to look stupid." Next time you encounter someone who is angry and unpleasant, try to imagine what their thought balloon might be saying. And if you feel the impulse to lash out or act unkindly, think about what your own thought balloon says. Try not to be governed by your fears.

Kindness in Action: *Are there people in your life who always seem to be angry and dissatisfied? People whom you avoid because they're such downers? Next time you encounter them, make an effort to turn them around with your kindness: focus on their fear or insecurity; think about how you might feel in their place. Are you that downer in somebody else's life? Be honest . . . you don't have to reveal your answer to anybody else. But if you have ever been a "Nasty Nancy," think about why, and whether it's resulted in peace and pleasure. What does the thought balloon above your head say when you're feeling stressed, tired, or somehow threatened?*

Chapter 13:

Dancing with Discovery: Taking Time to Notice the Kindness in Your Life

"Love doesn't mean doing extraordinary or heroic things. It means knowing how to do ordinary things with tenderness."
(Jean Vanier)

You may be reading this book as weekly meditations on kindness. Or you may be reading it over the course of a few sittings. Or you may simply be picking it up *whenever* and reading *wherever*. Whatever works for you is what works for you.

I hope you will pause periodically to think about what you are reading and what you have been able to put into practice, as well as what you may be struggling with. And think about the kindnesses all around you. Are you noticing them more? Are you seeing more opportunities you may have to extend kindness—to others and to yourself?

During my year of living kindly, I gave myself quarterly "report cards," measuring my progress and my shortcomings.

Looking back, I don't think it was the kindest way to assess my advancement toward my goals (a few of the people following my blog thought so, too!). But, nonetheless, there was some merit to the undertaking: I wanted to be mindful of my intentions, and I wanted to see if there were places in my life where kindness had really made a home, or others where I consistently fell short. I wanted to celebrate my progress and think about where I felt stuck. I hope you will want to do the same . . . kindly, of course.

Think about what you've read thus far and the ideas that have been sparked by your reading. What especially resonated for you? Where did you say to yourself "Aha!" or "Yes!" or even "Hmmmm"? Where are your kindness hot spots: in your car, in crowded stores, when you're traveling, or when you're in a hurry? Who are the people you find it easy to be kind to, and the ones who are not so easy, who always seem to push your buttons?

Do you tend to be judgy when confronted with behaviors that seem rude or inconsiderate? Have you tried to seek alternative explanations for such behaviors?

Your kindness "radar" may be operating on high right now, so you may be noticing more kindness around you, and also more unkindness. That awareness is key to moving forward. Just as you want to reduce your judgment of others, don't judge yourself. You're doing the best you can. Give yourself credit for the kindnesses you've extended and for your desire to be part of making a kinder world.

Set some intentions for the next few weeks. Be realistic. You're not suddenly going to become the next Mother Teresa, but where in your life can you offer a bit more kindness? For those situations that apply to you, can you:

- Back off the accelerator when another driver wants to merge into your lane?
- Wave thanks to a driver who gives way for you?
- Offer the benefit of the doubt to the shopper who blocks the aisle, gabs on his cell phone, or takes forever to write a check at the cash register?

- See someone's rudeness as an expression of their fear in a new and unfamiliar situation?
- Wash your partner's or your colleague's dirty dish without resentment and without lecturing them about cleaning up after themselves?
- Practice exerting the power of the pause? Swallow your words when feelings might be hurt, or when you're about to participate in gossip or unkind banter? Use that brief pause to look for a kinder explanation or determine the response that is most likely to bring peace?
- Let go of tracking who's ahead and who owes whom, and choose peace instead?
- Remind yourself of the many health benefits of kindness? While kindness is its own reward, being deliberate in our choice of kindness, and of positive over negative, offers the bonus of improved health.
- Try overcoming discomfort in social situations by focusing on alleviating another person's discomfort?
- Be intentional about the "germs" you want to spread or absorb from others, understanding that both kindness and unkindness are contagious?
- See the power of kindness in your workplace, and how compassion and encouragement enhance productivity, morale, and effectiveness?

What else can you do to embrace kindness? What will you do today?

PART TWO:

The Season
of Understanding

I. Barriers to Kindness

Chapter 14:

When Fear Gets in the Way of Kindness

"Be not afraid. A kind life, a life of spirit, is fundamentally a life of courage—the courage simply to bring what you have, to bring who you are." (Wayne Muller)

There are many barriers to extending kindness, and fear may be one of the biggest. Sometimes just the thought of putting myself out there or taking the risk to do something kind and face an unknown response can be enough to stifle the impulse. My kindness might be clumsy, it might be misinterpreted, it might be rejected. It's safer to do nothing.

I was attending a conference in Washington, DC, a few years back. A colleague and I were walking to a restaurant for dinner after a long day of meetings. We were stopped on the sidewalk by a young man who asked if we could spare any change to help him out. I reached into my wallet and handed him a couple of dollars. He walked on and so did we.

However, for the remainder of our walk and well into our dinner, my friend scolded me for giving the man money.

She said he was probably a freeloader who didn't want to work and made a living conning and begging tourists and bleeding hearts like me. How did I know that he was really in need, or that he wouldn't spend the money on drugs or alcohol? She said I was just making the problem worse by handing him money on the street. If he was really in need, there were social service agencies that could help. She told me I was a pushover and an easy mark. I was surprised by her vehemence—she was a very nice person, she was a nurse, for heaven's sake! I may have tried to defend my action, but mostly I was just embarrassed. Not embarrassed to have given money, but embarrassed to be scolded like a schoolgirl. Needless to say, if we were approached again by anyone on the walk back to our hotel—which I don't recall—that panhandler would have come up empty-handed.

I am somewhat chagrined to admit that since that evening I rarely give anyone money when I am accompanied by someone—whether it's a friend, my husband, or a business colleague. I'm afraid of an embarrassing scene or scolding such as the one in Washington, DC. I'm not proud that I have allowed my fear to inhibit my kindness. I've even rationalized it to some degree: this way, when I give someone money, I tell myself that I am freer to stop and exchange a few words with the individual and I don't have to feel rushed or worry that I'm delaying my companion. It is a rationalization, though. I'm afraid I will be scolded. Afraid I'll be embarrassed.

Just as fear can inhibit us from offering kindness, it can also be the impetus for our acting unkindly. Remember "Nasty Nancy," the unhappy conference attendee in Chapter 12? Her anger and complaints were largely the result of her fears in a new, overwhelming, and somewhat intimidating situation. Much of her unpleasant behavior dissipated when she was offered kindness and was able to admit her anxiety.

When I see unkindness—my own or others'—I can often trace it to fear: fear of judgment, fear of rejection, fear of the unknown, fear of not being enough, fear of being vulnerable or looking foolish. Many of the things we fear are also threats to our pride, to the image we have of how good, strong, smart, capable, and lovable we are. When these are shaken, we often strike out or strike back.

Sometimes, if we are able to see someone's unkindness toward us as an expression of their own fear, it is easier to forgive and respond to them with kindness, rather than retaliating and escalating the encounter.

Two Sides of One Coin

It's often said that when dealing with fears we should ask, "What is the worst that could happen?" Then, assuming the worst is not a fiery death or a lengthy prison term, we can further evaluate whether we could handle it. In the case of extending a kindness, what's the worst that could happen?

- I might be embarrassed. *I could deal with that—it won't be the first time.*
- I might be rejected. *I can get over that; I always have.*
- I might do it badly (whatever it is). *Well, that's how we learn—very few of us get "it" right the first time. But if we never try . . .*
- I might be judged as foolish, stupid, or weak. *Well, so whom does judgment reflect on, really? The judger, not me.*
- I might be put in a vulnerable position. *Well, that's not such a bad thing, is it? Vulnerability opens us up and helps us grow.*

I think it's a useful exercise to ask, "What's the worst that could happen?" But I also think that's only one side of the coin. The other side offers us the more important question: "What's the *best* that could happen?" Let's look at our potential action from that perspective: What's the best that could happen if I extend a kindness?

- I might help someone feel good or make it through a tough day.

- I might grow closer to an old friend or make a new one.
- My words or actions might be just what someone else needs to extend a kindness themselves.
- I might be appreciated.
- I might be regarded as loving, compassionate, or wise.
- I might become more confident in my own values and actions.
- I might overcome a fear and be the better person I want to be.
- I might change the world.

This last one might sound a bit grand, but, truly, we have no idea where or how far our kindnesses reverberate. The small kindness I extend to one person might cause them to extend a kindness they might not otherwise have acted upon. And then that person might extend a kindness, and . . . you get the picture. We've all heard the stories of someone suffering the depths of despair whose potential act of self-destruction was suspended by a seemingly small act—a kind note, or word, or gesture from someone. What if we approached every encounter with a sense of the sacredness of our words and actions, and of the potential each of us carries to change the world for the better? I think looking at *the best that could happen* is a great way to overcome the fear that keeps us from being kind to others, and perhaps also to ourselves.

Plus, if we're focused on *best*, rather than *worst*, then our eyes are on the prize—we're thinking about what we want to happen, not what we don't want. The world and our own unconscious inner resources will conspire to make it happen. It requires a change in our perspective and our paradigms. It may not be easy, but it's worth it. After, all, what's the worst that could happen . . . and what's the best?

Kindness in Action: *Think of a time when you experienced or witnessed unkindness. Could fear have been at the heart of it? Can you think of an instance where fear or a threat to your pride caused you to respond unkindly or to hesitate to extend a kindness? Can you recall what you were afraid of? Next time fear stops you, acknowledge the fear and ask yourself what's the worst that could happen, and then what's the best that could happen. Focus on the best!*

Chapter 15:

When We Don't Have Time

for Kindness

"We become what we love. Whatever you are giving your time and attention to, day after day, is the kind of person you will eventually become." (Wayne Muller)

Time seems to be our most precious resource these days. We all have the same twenty-four hours, but for most of us, it's never enough. There's rarely adequate time to do everything we want to do. And using some of that precious time to extend kindness may not seem a priority.

More and more, people seem to be valuing time above money. Surveys of employees indicate that it's more important to them to have life balance than a higher paycheck. Many nonprofit organizations are finding it difficult to recruit volunteers—prospects tell them they don't have the time, they'd rather spend the limited time they do have with their families. They'd rather make a financial donation than a contribution of time. Many of us justify our inactivity by deferring involvement until we have more time: *I'll get involved when the kids are older, when my job slows down, when I retire . . .*

The allocation of our time is an important decision, one involving the prioritization of all the obligations and options open to us. As writer Annie Dillard says, "How we spend our days is, of course, how we spend our lives."

With that in mind, as we allocate our time, are we creating space for kindness? If it's a priority, we will. But, it's a choice we need to make consciously, otherwise it may be squeezed out by the myriad other things clamoring for our time and attention.

It takes time to be kind:

- It takes time to pause and think about what is the kind response.
- It takes time to step out of our routine and enter into a genuine conversation, or provide assistance when doing so might delay us from our appointed rounds.
- It takes time to be patient—to allow others to fumble, stumble, and learn—without jumping in to fix, show them how to "do it right," or simply do it for them.
- It takes time to reach into our pocket and find a couple of dollars that might help someone make it through another day, and then to look that person in the eye and say a kind word.
- It takes time even to be kind to ourselves—to stop and think about what we need most at this moment—perhaps to slow down, take a walk, relax . . .

There was a time in my career when I was consistently working sixty-five to seventy-five hours a week, and also trying to maintain some sort of a life outside of work. I know now that I sometimes blew off opportunities to be kind. The few moments it would take to drop someone a note, or to go out of my way to pick up a small gift, or to invite a friend to lunch, or to bake a treat for a neighbor . . . all were just too much, like dumping a bathtub full of water into an already sinking rowboat. So I passed up opportunities to be kind and pushed away thoughts of what I might be missing.

I have friends and colleagues whose workloads were as crazy as mine who nonetheless made time to be kind. Their kindness and their priorities fill me with awe. What great examples they are. These are people who are just naturally kind, and who would probably think it unnecessary to set an intention of kindness, or to spend time pondering the nature of kindness. To them, kindness is like breathing; it requires no thought.

Kindness isn't something we do only when we have time for it. Kindness is how we choose to live. I'm reminded of Robert Corin Morris's lovely quote: "The way we live our life is our spiritual practice—no more, no less, nothing but, nothing else."

Once I cut my workload, I became much more aware of those opportunities I used to overlook, and I saw that fitting them into my previous life might have been just what I needed—for kindness is energizing. And enormously satisfying. Isn't it curious how many great lessons we learn through our rearview mirrors? It may not always be a *good* time to extend kindness, but it's almost always the *right* time.

Even if you really cannot squeeze one more thing into your day without setting off an explosion or collapsing into a heap, what you *can* do is make sure kindness is present in all of your current activities—big and small. Whether you are writing a note to your kid's teacher, managing a complex business or project, juggling two jobs, or caring for an elderly family member, you can do it kindly. Think of kindness as an accessory you always wear; let it become the trademark by which people recognize you.

There are many barriers to kindness, but I have come to see that when I make kindness a natural, first response, the barriers begin to crumble. Once I no longer have to tell myself to pause, to engage, to connect, kindness becomes second nature. Time and I still skirmish occasionally. And I remind myself daily that taking time for kindness is what gives meaning to life. But it's more than just "taking time for kindness": kindness isn't something we slip into our behavior when time permits;

kindness must become the way we do things. That's when we will have become kind people.

 Kindness in Action: *Do you often feel the pressure of not enough time and too much to do? Have you passed up opportunities to extend kindness because you felt you didn't have time? In retrospect, would the time needed truly have inconvenienced you, or might it have provided a welcome boost of energy or appreciation? Can you envision a time when kindness becomes a top priority in your life? Maybe it already is. Recognizing that family, career, education, social and community activities and commitments—no matter how rewarding or enjoyable—can take up nearly all of our waking hours, how can you approach all of these with a spirit of kindness? Try scheduling some kindness in your life—maybe a half hour every Sunday afternoon to write a few notes to friends or relatives whom you rarely see. Donate blood regularly, or volunteer for a cause you believe in. And don't forget self-kindness. Over dinner with your family, plan something kind you can all do together next weekend. You'll never regret making time for kindness.*

Chapter 16:

I Don't Have the Patience for This!

"The more you know yourself, the more patience you have for what you see in others." (Erik Erikson)

At our local grocery store, we sometimes see a sign at certain checkout stands: "Checker in Training." It's a gentle way of saying, *"If you're in a hurry, this isn't the line for you."* As a result, people tend to avoid those lines. A lot of people don't have the patience to wait while the novice checker searches for bar codes or looks up the code for every produce item. Or while she laboriously bags the groceries, or calls her supervisor for help replacing the register ribbon. I used to avoid those lines, too. One day, it occurred to me that a simple kindness would be to get in line where a checker is training, and encourage him or her by simply being patient. So I do that. I smile and I say, "Take your time."

If they're nervous or apologetic for the delays, I remark, "I'm in no hurry, you're doing great." And when my groceries are packed up and I'm heading out, I'll say, "Thank you! You were terrific!" The checker is beaming and the person who was behind me in line picks up the mantle of patience and kindness.

Just as time is a barrier to kindness, so is impatience. The two are related, but there's a difference.

I've never been a particularly patient person. In a meeting, I want speakers to get to the point; I often skip over paragraphs of flowery description in books to get to the action or the dialogue; when people kept me waiting, I used to fidget and fume. As I focused on kindness, I found myself becoming more patient, and that significantly altered my outlook.

Impatience may be the result of feeling one doesn't have time for the chitchat, or time to be kept on hold. After all, our lives are overflowing with obligations, deadlines, and activities—leading to anxiety to move on to the next thing or to avoid wasting time. In the face of disappearing time, kindness may not always be a priority.

If we are in a hurry, taking time to say kind words, offer assistance, or extend ourselves will just slow us down more. We'll fall further behind. Sometimes it feels like the more rushed we are, the more things seem to be conspiring to get in our way: the slowest line at the post office, the driver who is stuck in first gear, the acquaintance who wants to tell us in great detail how she selected the yarn for the sweater she is knitting for her dog. Yikes, we don't have time for this! They'll understand if we blow them off . . . after all, we're busy!

But what is it we're rushing to? Often, it's our job, a meeting, the next obligation on our never-ending list. How many of us are so important or so overscheduled that we really haven't time to be kind? And if that's the case, what's wrong with this picture? If we are that important or overscheduled, is it by our choice, or someone else's, or maybe nobody's—we just think that's the way it's supposed to be?

What if we changed our perspective? Instead of allowing ourselves to get impatient because of our jobs, what if being kind was our number one job?

If being kind is my most important job, won't it be easier to stand in line at the grocery store while the person in front of me fumbles for her checkbook and questions the cashier about the price of asparagus? Won't it be easier to follow the car going twenty-five miles an hour when the speed limit is forty-five? Won't it be easier to wait through fifteen minutes of "hold" music for the next customer service representative, or to listen to my neighbor tell me something she finds fascinating, even if I don't? *It's all part of the job.*

There are other circumstances in which we may have all the *time* in the world, but we don't have much tolerance for the circumstances we find ourselves in.

We also find ourselves losing patience when someone else can't do something as quickly or proficiently as we can. We may have plenty of time but lack the tolerance for patience or kindness. Embarrassing admission: I was really late in learning to tie my shoes, *really* late. Most of my friends had that skill down when they were four or five. I was still struggling at seven. It wasn't that I didn't want to learn, but my parents quickly discovered that teaching me wasn't easy, and it was a lot easier just to tie my shoes for me, or to buy me shoes that didn't need tying. The problem was that I was left-handed and everyone else in my family was right-handed. They'd show me how they did it, but I couldn't make my hands do what theirs did. Then they'd try to figure out how to do it from a left-handed perspective, and they couldn't do it. So, the heck with it, just tie the kid's shoes for her and send her on her way.

Finally, my mom or my dad found someone who was left-handed and asked him to show me. With a few repetitions and a bit of patience, the learning came easily and, happily for all, I've been tying my own shoes quite successfully for many decades.

There are also things that require our patience that we simply cannot muster the enthusiasm or interest for.

Perhaps it's a child's description of his encyclopedic love of dinosaurs, or a spouse's explanation of quantum mechanics and wave-particle duality (yep, my husband). The kind response is not to roll our eyes or look at our watch. Listen with interest. Even if you can't relate to—or understand—what they are saying, you can appreciate their enthusiasm and encourage their interest. We learn complex concepts by explaining them to others, so even if as a listener we don't understand or care, the gift of our listening helps the speaker cement their own knowledge and understanding. If nothing else, we hold the space for that person to talk and share—and what a fine gift that is!

My point here is that regardless of time issues, patience is required when it comes to teaching and to learning. The best parents, teachers, and managers know that they need to allow the learner to stumble, fumble, or even just sit and think about it—without jumping in to fix, show them how to "do it right," or do it for them. My husband tutors kids in math and science; I see this patient kindness in his teaching. If one explanation doesn't do the trick, Bill finds another, or asks just the right questions until the students get it themselves. He never rushes them or shows impatience, and when they finally get a concept, they *own* it.

Sometimes, we may think we're being kind when we rush in to help, or to fix, or to get it *just right*, but what we may be doing is disempowering the person we think we're helping. The truly kind response may be to stand by silently while they figure it out, or to explain a concept again in a different way, or to be willing to show someone something for the tenth time. Or perhaps to give them the space to figure something out at their own pace. All of these responses require patience. Too often, as an employer, I told myself it was just easier to do it myself than to show an employee how to do something, or to wait for them to get it right. I am learning, though, that exercising patience helps my employee become more capable and ultimately reduces my workload. There's a gift in patience, if we just take the time to look for it.

It takes patience to be kind and kindness to be patient. But if I can view being kind as my job, it will be much easier to patiently teach a child, or instruct a new employee in an unfamiliar skill, or refrain from jumping in and doing something myself, thus denying someone else the opportunity to contribute, as well as a valuable growth lesson.

Kindness in Action: *Do you miss opportunities to be kind because you are just too impatient to pause and give the gift of your time and attention? How would you view your schedule differently if you elevated kindness to a top priority? Have there been times when you've stepped in to finish a task or commandeer a project because you were frustrated by the time it was taking your child, spouse, employee, or colleague to master the necessary skills? Again, could you respond differently if you viewed extending kindness and patience as your job, or an essential part of it? Think about your body language, too: Do you roll your eyes, look at your watch, reach for your cell phone? Where and how might you experiment with this new perspective on patience?*

Chapter 17:

Other Barriers to Kindness

"I expect to pass through life but once. If, therefore, there be any kindness I can show, or any good thing I can do to any fellow being, let me do it now, and not defer or neglect it, as I shall not pass this way again." (William Penn)

As I continue to explore kindness, I see that certain elements keep appearing—consistent pathways to kindness and persistent barriers to kindness. Taking time to recognize the obstacles may help us avoid them and strategize in advance how to overcome such barriers. We've talked about fear, time pressures, and impatience. Here are a few more factors that might keep us from being our best self.

Laziness and Inertia

While there are certainly kind actions we can take that don't require a lot of energy (a smile, a compliment, a door held open), many kindnesses do require that we extend ourselves. They require that we get off our butts, go out of our way, and sometimes even leave our comfort zones. Usually it's just a matter of taking the first step and then our intentions take over and kindness ensues. But the hurdle is that first step and overcoming the inertia to take it.

Indifference

We talked about this earlier, too (in Chapter 4). The antithesis of kindness, indifference is a barrier to living a kind life. One cannot be kind if caring is absent; one cannot be kind if one is willing to shrug and say, "It's not my problem." Indifference may be how we protect ourselves from strong feelings, from the caring that moves us to action. It may be comfortable to wallow in indifference, but kindness requires that we stop being a spectator and jump into life.

Entitlement

Sadly, there are many people who see kindness—if they see it at all—as something that is optional and depends upon the situation and the status of the people involved. It's not as essential to show kindness to the clerk, the cashier, or the homeless person as it is to the VIP who can help one get ahead or feel powerful. The person who cuts in line, the one who parks in the handicapped space without a permit to save a few steps—somehow, they adopted the false notion that they are superior and thus deserving of more or finer than other people. They expect kindness from others but rarely think that the equation goes both ways. Selective kindness isn't kindness; it's opportunism. Kindness is something we extend to everyone at every opportunity.

Obliviousness

It's easy to miss opportunities to be kind if we aren't paying attention to what's going on around us. We may not notice that there is a person behind us for whom we can hold a door, or that someone needs help carrying their groceries, or that a child is frightened or sad. Too often, we allow technology to take precedence over human connection—we are constantly absorbed in our devices, oblivious to the life around us and the myriad opportunities we have to offer the gift of our kindness. We can even be oblivious to our own need for self-care—unaware that we have depleted our energy and need to engage in some personal renewal if we want to be able to care for others. Living consciously and being actively attentive is easier said than done, but it's one of the essential elements of a kind life.

Habit

If we are in the habit of saying no, it's hard to say yes—to someone who asks for assistance, for our time, or for a dollar or two to help make it through the day. Of course, we can't say yes to everything or everyone, but whichever answer we choose should come out of conscious conviction rather than robotic routine. Here again, a kind life asks us to stay awake.

Fatigue

Research has shown that when we're overtired, we're more prone to accidents, we feel stressed, and we have difficulty learning and being creative. On top of that, we are also more likely to commit unethical or unkind acts. As we try to squeeze too much into our already overscheduled lives, many of us forego adequate sleep, unaware of its many health benefits and the need we have for daily replenishment. America is often referred to as a sleep-deprived nation. It makes me wonder just how much of the bad behavior we see and read about daily is attributable to tired people intersecting with other tired people and neither making the best choices. I know from my own experience that when I'm especially tired I'm not as kind as when I am rested and refreshed. It's not that I am overtly unkind—though I've been known to be snappish when drowsy—but I bypass opportunities to extend kindness. I'm just too tired. Or maybe I'm just operating on autopilot. Whatever it is, when weary it's harder to summon the energy for kindness. As I've gotten older, I've come to value sleep more than ever—and knowing that it helps make me kinder just makes my bed even warmer and cozier.

There's another kind of fatigue that can be a barrier to kindness. Compassion fatigue is a type of stress caused by too much caring for others. It often leads to burnout when the empathy required to constantly be caring for and helping others becomes too much. That's why both professional and family caregivers need to understand that they must occasionally step back, even step away, and take care of themselves. For some, that's very hard to do. They feel selfish; they fear judgment. But as the Dalai Lama advises: "For the sake of everyone . . . withdraw and restore yourself. The point is to have a long-term perspective." It can also be a matter of reframing the efforts that exhaust us—looking at them through a lens of kindness or serving, rather than managing and helping. Martyrdom is a heavy weight.

A less obvious kind of compassion fatigue is what we feel after lengthy and constant bombardment of distressing news. If we are fed a daily diet of news about crime, poverty, oppression, terrorism, corporate malfeasance, and incivility, after a while despair settles in, and we might feel a loss of hope that there's any place for kindness in the world. After a while, we just stop feeling anything when we hear of another shooting, another crooked politician, or another starving child. Adopting the long view, as the Dalai Lama recommends, means that taking care of ourselves—whether it's declaring a news fast, taking a walk, or calling a friend and going to the movies—might sometimes be the kindest response we can make.

There will always be obstacles to kindness. Being aware of what might get in the way of our kindness makes us more able to sidestep or overcome them.

Kindness in Action: *This is my list, but I suspect the barriers to kindness are similar for most of us. Have I left anything out? When you miss an opportunity to be kind, can you ascribe it to any of the above, or are there other reasons? Think about how you can become more aware of the particular barriers that get in the way of your kindness. And when you do see them, how can you get past them? Think proactively about how you will respond next time you face an obstacle to being your best self. Plan a small reward for jumping that hurdle and putting needed kindness out into the world. If you don't already, get adequate sleep (for most of us that's seven to eight hours) every night for two weeks and see if it makes any difference. Plan ahead that next time someone asks you for something that you have always automatically said no to, you will say yes, and commit to that yes wholeheartedly.*

II. Resistance to Kindness

Chapter 18:

Rejecting Kindness

"We do not actually know other people; we only know our judgments." (Bryant McGill)

I don't like rejection. Who does, right? A work colleague seemed to be having a very bad day. She was clearly unhappy and had spoken sharply to me and a couple of other people in our office. I wanted to be kind. I tapped on the wall of her cubicle and said, "Are you okay? You seem to be having a bad day. Can I help with anything?"

She looked at me, pain clearly in her eyes, and said, "Yes, you can leave me alone."

Ouch! I put my arms up and backed away. Was there more I could have done or said? I don't know. I think I had probably been pretty clumsy in my effort. It didn't feel good to have my attempt at kindness rejected, but I had tried. I hesitated, though, before offering my help to her again.

It can be upsetting and bewildering when someone rejects our kindness. An act that was meant to be helpful and benign is rebuffed. Sometimes, the intended recipient even lashes out at us. What did we do wrong? Are we in some way at fault, or inadequate?

As a result, the next time we want to extend a kindness, we hesitate—fearing rejection or scorn. Our act of kindness dies before it is born.

There is a simple saying that I use often in working with groups or in one-on-one situations: *We assume one another's good intent.* So simple and yet so powerful. If only we could always remember it!

The *Seattle Times* runs a daily section called "Rant and Rave." It invites readers to share examples of good and bad behavior and positive and negative encounters in our community. The raves are frequently descriptions of generosity and kindnesses experienced and witnessed—they're often uplifting and touching, little vignettes that reinforce our shared humanity. Here's an example: *"For the Men's Warehouse employees who helped my developmentally disabled son have the senior prom he'd dreamed of, and for his teachers who made it all happen. It was a night he'll never forget!"*

The rants, on the other hand, often describe careless, rude, or unscrupulous deeds or situations. A rant caught my eye: *"To the guy in the VW who flipped me the bird, mouthed obscenities through the glass, and then sped off when I was knocking on his window to let him know his tire was flat."*

Who knows why the driver reacted as he did. He may have been frightened, surprised, or embarrassed. He may have thought he was caught doing something naughty. He may have been having a lousy day, and the knock on his window put him over the edge. (If that's the case, the dawning awareness of a flat tire a short time later can't have added to the day's enjoyment.) But how sad it is that the first reaction some people have to unexpected contact by strangers is to strike out. Sadder still is the likelihood that the person who knocked on the car window will think twice before he or she does something like that again.

We've all heard of road rage precipitated by a honking horn when someone fails to notice the light has turned green. A tap on the horn is a kindness under those circumstances, one to be responded to with a wave of thanks as the driver proceeds through the light. Too often it initiates an angry gesture, a curse, or even a brandished weapon.

For those reasons, we are often wary. I've seen lines of cars patiently waiting through two green lights for the oblivious driver to notice that the light has changed. (I live in Seattle, where we tend to be boundlessly courteous.) Rather than honk, I once saw a man get out of his car and politely tap on the driver's window of the car ahead. For his effort, he was rewarded with an unkind gesture and screech of tires as the driver shot through the now-yellow light. I'm sure the driver was embarrassed, but what is it about embarrassment that makes some of us lash out?

As the recipient of a kind gesture, we may be embarrassed that our need was perceived, that we might appear weak or incompetent. As the extender of kindness, we might be embarrassed by the response it kindles—whether rejection, gratitude, confusion, or stony silence. There have been times, I admit, when I chose not to extend a kindness because I feared the response: I didn't want to draw attention to myself, I thought the people I was with would disapprove, or I feared the reaction from the intended recipient. I regret that I didn't listen to my first impulse and pull out my wallet, lend a hand, or say the words that came to my mind. I sometimes attribute my reticence to shyness, but I see that my shyness is also often how I avoid potential embarrassment.

Embarrassment is part of the human experience. It's also what makes us human, whether an unzipped fly, a broccoli-adorned tooth, or a verbal gaffe. It happens. We've all been there. To not risk embarrassment is to shun human contact and live halfheartedly. It seems to me that grace is the ideal response to those embarrassing moments. More broadly, though, isn't grace the best response to almost anything?

I hope the person who knocked on the window of the VW isn't deterred from doing so the next time she thinks a stranger would want to know what she has noticed.

And I hope we all (myself most definitely included) can learn to react with grace when someone tries to help us.

Kindness in Action: *Think of a time when you rejected someone's kindness because you were embarrassed or unsure, or because it made you feel vulnerable or weak. Reenvision the situation and accept the kindness. How does that feel? How is the outcome of the situation or encounter changed? Can you also think of a time when you considered doing something kind but then withheld the gesture? What was the reason: fear, embarrassment, apathy, shyness . . . ? Reenvision that situation and pay attention to how you feel extending kindness, and how the recipient of your kindness may have responded and been helped by you. Think now about how you will respond next time an opportunity to give or receive kindness arises.*

Chapter 19:

On the Receiving End of Kindness

*"One who knows how to show and to accept kindness will be
a friend better than any possession." (Sophocles)*

Even if we don't have the resources to give all that we
would like to give, we always have the capacity to receive
graciously. It sounds so simple, but it can be surprisingly
hard. Think of the times someone tried to give you something and you demurred—perhaps because you didn't think
they could afford it, or you didn't feel worthy, or it was simply
your initial reaction to an awkward situation. Maybe the gift
wasn't something you wanted; perhaps you didn't want to feel
indebted. Or maybe you are among the cynical who wonder,
What's the catch?

Did your refusal of their offer please them, or did it disappoint? In retrospect, would a gracious "thank you" have made
both of you happier and immensely more comfortable?

In her lovely book *The Art of Grace*[1], Sarah Kaufman offers
the following advice: "Be easily pleased. Accept compliments,

take a seat on the bus if someone offers it to you, embrace any kindness that comes your way. This is graciousness, and it is a gift for someone else. You are giving another person the gift of being graceful."

Giving is such a pleasurable act. Yet we often deny our friends and acquaintances—and even strangers—the joy and satisfaction of giving by being such terrible receivers.

And the gift doesn't have to be something material. How often do we devalue the gift of others' words by refusing their compliments? We deflect kind words about our appearance by saying, "No, I look terrible! My hair's a mess and I really should lose ten pounds, and look, I've lost a button on this shirt." Do you really think they compliment us just to hear us point out all our flaws? I seriously doubt it.

How much better to respond with, "How nice of you to say so," or "Thanks for your kind words, they make me feel great!"

In his book *Imperfect Alternatives*[2], Dr. Dale Turner quotes a friend who chided him for brushing off a compliment: "When someone gives you a compliment in words, don't disagree or minimize what he says, for words are gifts, too. Accept them gratefully, even though you don't think you deserve them. . . . A compliment is a gift not to be thrown away carelessly unless you want to hurt the giver."

We also reject compliments on our achievements by downplaying them. We say, "No, it really wasn't anything special. Anybody could have done it. I was lucky." It's as if we are saying, *No, you dolt. Can't you see I'm really an incompetent bungler?* It's always great to share credit—that's another form of kindness (not to mention decency)—but minimizing the overall accomplishment serves no one.

How much better to say, "Thank you, I'm really pleased with the result, too," or "Yes! Don't we have a fabulous team!"

As I pose the question of why accepting compliments is something most of us aren't very good at, I realize this is a much larger issue for women than for men. When was the last time you complimented a man on his new suit and he responded by saying that it makes his butt look big? Doesn't happen.

Most of the men I interact with know how to accept compliments about their work. In fact, they expect kudos . . . and good for them for having those expectations. A lot of women, though, were raised with the direct or indirect instruction to hide their light under a bushel. Our mothers told us to be modest. Our teachers encouraged humility and restraint. Somebody else kept telling us that the meek would inherit the earth.

Perhaps if we reframe our response to gifts and compliments we can more easily receive them. Instead of questioning whether we deserve them, or fearing that we will appear conceited, or worrying that we are getting more than our share, let's stop thinking about ourselves and think instead about the giver and what response might please them most. Think about the kindness we can extend to them by accepting their gift with grace.

Kindness in Action: *Set an intention to embrace the kindnesses that come your way—in word and in deed—and to do so with genuine appreciation. Think about the last time you received a compliment—for work you did, for how you looked, or for an effort you made. How did you respond? Do you think your response made the complimenter feel good? Next time you are given a compliment—any compliment— receive it graciously. No demurring. No downplaying. No false modesty. In fact, how about setting an intention of receiving compliments graciously for the next twenty-one days and see how that feels? Try extending some compliments, too, authentic ones. That means paying attention and speaking up when you notice someone doing something right, or making an effort worthy of note. Who couldn't use a few well-chosen compliments?*

Chapter 20:

It All Starts with Kindness to Self

"Self-care is never a selfish act—it is simply good steward-ship of the only gift I have, the gift I was put on earth to offer others. Anytime we can listen to true self and give the care it requires, we do it not only for ourselves, but for the many others whose lives we touch." (Parker Palmer)

I can't effectively extend kindness to others or graciously receive kindness from them if I don't have a solid relationship of kindness with one very important person: me.

Seems obvious, but how often are we rather unkind to that person we live and breathe with 24/7? Sometimes we're downright abusive; other times, we're indifferent or neglectful.

I'm going to employ an overworked analogy here—one we encounter every time we take to the friendly skies: "Should there be a loss of cabin pressure, oxygen masks will drop from the overhead compartment. . . . *Be sure to secure your own mask before assisting others.*"

We've heard it a thousand times, and not just from our amiable flight attendant—it is part of the repertoire of every motivational speaker on the circuit. Yes, it's overworked and trite, but think about it in its original and literal setting: If you were a child or someone who might need assistance donning an oxygen mask, would you prefer to get that help from a person who is breathing calmly and offering assurance that this is a minor inconvenience that we will handle together, or from a wild-eyed martyr who may pass out at any moment?

And in more earthbound circumstances, I find it more pleasurable to receive a kindness from someone who is steady and self-assured than from someone whose attempt at kindness seems to be born more out of desperation or obligation than of genuine caring. And I find it easier to extend kindness to someone who is able to receive it than to someone who can't because they don't feel worthy.

There is not a one-size-fits-all method of being kind to ourselves. What works for some won't for others. Let's explore just a few.

Knowing When to Say Yes to Saying No

Saying yes to our own lives sometimes means knowing how to say no to others. When we give so much to others that we have nothing left to give ourselves, we must find ways to replenish our energy and restore our strength. Like a good runner, we must pace ourselves. Likewise, there are times when we need to speak a gentle "no" to ourselves, when we are poised to embark on a self-destructive action, or when we simply need permission to get off the merry-go-round.

Changing Our Self-Talk

How many of us say things to ourselves that we would never say to another human being? We call ourselves stupid, clumsy, ugly, fat. We criticize our slightest error. We tell ourselves that we don't deserve the good things that come our way and that we do deserve the bad. If we happen to look in the mirror and notice that the person looking back at us is looking pretty hot today, we immediately look for the flaw: *Check out that hair, brushed it with a cattle prod, did you?* We need to notice when we're engaging in verbal self-abuse and change it on the spot: *Dahling, you look magnificent! Come, let the world see how beautiful you are!*

Finding Our Own Satisfaction Triggers

Everybody has different self-care activators, and they are as diverse as the population is: reading, exercise, bubble baths, being in nature, listening to music, writing, walking the dog or petting the cat, romance, travel, swimming, tennis, meditation, spending time with friends, spending time alone. These are just a few. What are your satisfaction triggers? We all need to recognize the activities that replenish and reenergize us and then activate them with some frequency. If we don't take care of ourselves, who will?

Recognizing Boundaries

I look at boundaries as something like values. My friend Lynn describes values as "decisions we make in advance," and I think boundaries are much the same. They are the demarcation of what I will and will not do, and what I will and will not allow as I interact with others. They are both external and internal. External boundaries protect us from invasions of our space, our emotions and beliefs, and even our possessions. Internal boundaries help us manage our time, our emotions, and our impulses. Without a sense of our own boundaries we can deplete ourselves by trying excessively to please, serve, or fix, by tolerating abuse, by accepting criticism without evaluating it, by overscheduling our lives till we reach exhaustion, or by taking on other people's baggage. Learning to both establish and hold to our boundaries is a big element of self-kindness.

Forgiving

As someone who has done her share of stupid and thoughtless things, I have finally learned that continuing to carry them around with me in the form of regrets and self-recriminations serves no one . . . and it's a dreadfully heavy weight. That doesn't mean ignoring them but rather learning from them, forgiving myself, and letting them go. There is a quote of unknown origin that says it well: *Your past mistakes are meant to guide you, not define you.*

Small Indulgences

Somewhat related to satisfaction triggers, "small indulgences" is a term I first heard from trend-watcher Faith Popcorn[1]. She was referring to the tiny "affordable luxuries" that we allow ourselves—they don't break the budget, and they offer a quick and easy respite from stress. In the commercial world, Starbucks embodies small indulgences, having convinced us that the answer to our immediate need is a caramel macchiato, a chai tea, or simply a good cup of Ethiopian blend. But we can find small indulgences all around us: a piece of dark, artisan chocolate . . . a magazine we enjoy but don't usually spend five dollars to buy . . . a visit to a museum . . . a massage . . . just about anything by a couple of guys named Ben and Jerry . . . or maybe it's buying that new bestseller we've been wanting to read rather than waiting months to get it from the library. What's your favorite small indulgence?

The Dalai Lama has said: "For the sake of everyone . . . withdraw and restore yourself. The point is to have a long-term perspective." Good advice.

We need to be kind to ourselves if we are going to be able to give genuine kindness to others and to receive kindnesses. The challenge is to feel worthy and not to listen to that voice— ours now, but probably once that of a parent or teacher—that says putting ourselves first is always selfish. Selfish and unselfish is a polarity we must manage, recognizing that there are times when our need is greater and other times when someone else must come first, and still other times when putting someone else's need above our own *is* our greatest need.

For some, self-care may feel analogous to selfishness or self-absorption, and taken to an extreme, like anything else, it ceases to serve us. It's no fun spending time with someone who has nothing of interest to talk about but herself, or anyone above the age of eight who still believes that the universe revolves entirely around him. Yet those people are all around us, and they can be exhausting. We can't change them, but as a gesture of kindness to ourselves, we can limit our exposure to them.

The barriers that prevent us from being kind to ourselves are generally the same obstacles that keep us from being kind to others: time, fear, fatigue, apathy, obliviousness . . .

If we are to have a long-term perspective on compassion, as the Dalai Lama encourages, that means recognizing that kindness begins with self and radiates outward. Unless we replenish ourselves periodically, we cannot offer our gifts to others and to a universe that is in dire need of our kindness.

Kindness in Action: *Is your self-talk generally positive or negative? Practice thinking and saying things to yourself that are encouraging and compassionate. Ignore any voice that tells you you're not worthy. What are your satisfaction triggers? Your go-to small indulgence? How do you express kindness toward yourself? Are you carrying around regrets that serve no purpose other than to weigh you down? Thank them for the lessons they taught you and let them go. What's the kindest thing you could do for yourself right now? What's stopping you?*

Chapter 21:

No Kindness Is Ever Too Small

"On most days, the biggest thing you can do is a small act of kindness, decency, or love." (Cory Booker)

Have you ever bypassed opportunities to extend kindness because they're just too puny? *Just* writing a quick note to express appreciation for a colleague's wise advice, or *just* offering some leftover soup and store-bought bread to a neighbor—these things seem so small. Insignificant really. If I were *really* kind, I would send flowers to my colleague, or bake fresh bread for my neighbor. If I am to be a caring and compassionate person, I must express my kindness through grand gestures. Right?

Not so much.

While there's nothing wrong with grand gestures, a kind life is composed of the myriad ordinary, day-to-day kindnesses that may seem small but accumulate like sand upon the shore.

I recently came across the notion of TNTs, or "tiny noticeable things," an idea promulgated by British speaker Adrian Webster[1]. TNTs are those small and simple actions we take that brighten the lives of the people with whom we interact. A TNT is a smile, a word of appreciation, an offer of assistance, or the genuine interest we have for the people in our lives. None of these actions are grand or earth-moving, but cumulatively they change moods, change lives, and maybe even can change the world.

Along the same lines, MIT Professor Mary Rowe coined the term "micro-affirmations"[2] when she was serving as the university's ombudsman in the 1970s. Her job was to address bias against minorities, women, and people with disabilities in the MIT workplace. She described the importance of micro-affirmations, those "tiny acts of opening doors to opportunity, gestures of inclusion and caring, and graceful acts of listening. Micro-affirmations lie in the practice of generosity, in consistently giving credit to others—in providing comfort and support when others are in distress. . . ."

She also identified what she termed "micro-inequities." These are "apparently small events which are often ephemeral and hard to prove, events which are covert, often unintentional, frequently unrecognized by the perpetrator, which occur wherever people are perceived to be 'different.'" Examples might include failing to introduce the participants at a meeting, being too busy to greet a colleague or welcome a guest, making an assumption about a person because of their race or gender, perhaps unintentionally making an insensitive comment. They have a cumulative corrosive effect.

While these terms were originally used to discuss workplace inequality and bias, I believe the concept applies equally to kindness. Let's call them micro-kindnesses and micro-unkindnesses.

Think about the micro-unkindnesses we encounter daily. We often recognize them by the resigned sigh they evoke in us: a colleague's scowl, the neighbor who fails to pick up his dog's poop on your lawn, the long delay for which no explanation or apology is given.

Maybe we're guilty of micro-unkindnesses ourselves, thinking it really doesn't matter if we fail to greet our coworkers in the morning, or if we don't acknowledge the driver who slowed so we could merge into her lane. Such trifling actions don't really matter, do they? *Oh, yes, they do!*

Micro-kindnesses are often recognized by our spontaneous smile and accompanying warm feelings: a friendly greeting by the barista or bank teller, the colleague who steps in to help without being asked, the neighbor who shares the bounty from his vegetable garden.

While micro-kindnesses are often related to our interactions with others, they can also be things we do alone: picking up and disposing of trash when we take a walk, rolling the abandoned shopping cart from the parking lot back to the store, feeding a couple of quarters into an expired parking meter. Maybe they don't feel like much, but imagine a world where such actions were standard operating procedure for most of us.

Like nearly everything that matters in life, micro-kindnesses will grow if we pay attention. If we allow ourselves to be awake and aware—and not completely absorbed by our devices or our tendency to wander into oblivion—we will notice all the little things that call to us: the child in the supermarket who wants us to notice the funny faces he is making (and make a face back at him), the person ahead of us whose hands are too full to open the door, even the small kindness we may need to give ourselves—a few moments of quiet, a walk around the block if we have been sitting too long at our desk.

 ***Kindness in Action:** Take one day to simply pay attention to how many micro-kindnesses you extend in a day. Notice, also, if you succumb to a few micro-unkindnesses. Keep a rough tally and let that number be your baseline. Then each day for the next week or longer, see if you can increase the number of micro-kindnesses and decrease the micro-unkindnesses. You'll need to keep paying attention. As you notice places where your small acts of kindness are needed, do them. Try to keep track. If counting kindnesses seems just too compulsive and stresses you, don't count, just pay attention. If it*

feels like you are doing more little kindnesses each day, then you are, and good for you. Ideally, you'll like extending small kindnesses so much you'll simply continue the practice, getting ever better at it. Pretty soon, these micro-kindnesses will become second nature, and you'll be seeing opportunities—large and small—to extend your kindness everywhere. Little things do mean a lot!

III. Opening Our Lives to Kindness

Chapter 22:

Kindness and Abundance:

Enough *Is* Enough!

"True kindness is rooted in a deep sense of abundance, out of which flows a sense that even as I give, it is being given back to me." (Wayne Muller)

It's easier to be kind when we have the sense of abundance that Wayne Muller describes above. If we are always worrying that there won't be enough, or that if I share what I have with you, there will not be enough for me, it is hard to extend kindness.

Have you ever felt resentment or envy toward someone who experienced good fortune or great success? Maybe you found yourself rationalizing it *("Well, sure, with his family connections, getting that job was easy")*, or minimizing it *("What's the big deal? So she got a MacArthur Genius Grant—they're a dime a dozen")*. Or maybe you noticed the grinding of your molars as you congratulated someone for their success.

Thoughts like that are focused on scarcity: if *she* gets a lot, there will be less for me.

The world offers us two perspectives on abundance.

Cultural anthropologist Jennifer James often speaks about the concept of the limited or unlimited pie[1]. If we view our world as a limited pie, our slice is smaller if someone else gets a big piece. But if we can see the pie as unlimited—expanding endlessly from the center—then we have no reason to feel threatened or diminished by someone else's success or prosperity: there's plenty for everyone, and the size of mine isn't affected by the size of yours.

Rarely does someone else's abundance mean a dearth for us. It doesn't work that way. Success and good fortune—like sunshine—are not rationed. There's an ample supply for everybody. In fact, the more we all recognize the bounty surrounding us, the more there is for everyone, because—through kindness and our own contentment—we start helping others to experience abundance. We share what we have because, after all, there's plenty. And, like a boomerang or an eager puppy, it bounds right back to us.

This doesn't mean kind people never experience envy and pettiness. They're as susceptible as the rest of us, but perhaps more able to acknowledge and move beyond those feelings quickly.

For the rest of us, on those days when we wake up feeling *less than*, it is easy to lose sight of what really matters. That's when a sense of abundance needs to be summoned. It supports both our internal and external views of our world. Maybe we feel less than attractive, or less than smart, or less than capable, or less than secure. Or maybe we are aware that we don't have the wealth or resources that others do. Focusing on what we don't have—whether real or imagined—only ignites a downward spiral.

While trite, it is the old "glass half-full or half-empty" conundrum. We create our own reality by how we look at the world. If we view it through the lens of "not enough," that is what we train ourselves to look for, and we are never satisfied. If we view it through the lens of abundance, then how easy it is to be satisfied and to see that there is enough to share.

Without a sense of abundance, we can neither give nor receive. We hold our own possessions too tightly, and we have neither the open eyes nor the open hands to see and receive all that the world is offering us.

To believe we have enough, we must first believe we *are* enough. We are surrounded, though, by messages that tell us we are not. These are messages of a different kind of abundance: the copious consumption and assiduous acquisition that are so prevalent in Western society.

Even if we're lucky enough to have family and friends who see us as whole and perfect just as we are, the media bombards us with messages that we're not. Magazines show us the fashions we're lacking, or the youthful skin that we've lost. Television shows us—both through advertising and Hollywood's relatively narrow view of beauty—that we're far from adequate: some bits are too small and some are too big, our clothes lack style, our hair lacks luster, but, *good news*, there's a product to fix all our faults. Ads about weight, skin, and hair plague us online and continually remind us that there's a wonder drug or serum just waiting to solve our problems.

We are subtly and not so subtly taught to believe in our own inadequacy: we are not enough; something is missing. And the solution is always *out there*—something that will fix us or make us whole. If we just buy the right stuff, acquire the missing magic ingredient . . . If we allow it to, it becomes an endless quest for *more*. Embracing abundance provides a satisfaction that quells any need for comparison, envy, or feelings of inadequacy.

The view of abundance we see from the lens of kindness tells us we have what we need to live a life of joy and meaning and service, and we are fine just as we are. The commoditizing view of abundance whispers to us that we aren't enough and need to acquire more to be adequate. We hear them both . . . which voice resonates more deeply with you? Which will you choose to listen to?

Kindness in Action: *Think about why it's sometimes difficult to see someone else's success or wealth without feeling a pang of envy or feeling somehow diminished. Does your own worldview tend to be one of abundance or one of scarcity? Can you recall where those messages came from? How about the messages that tell you you're imperfect—that you need to be more or less than you are at this moment? Next time an image or commercial message instills in you the thought that you need something they're selling to make you whole, think about how that message was crafted and what hooked you. Then gently but firmly unhook yourself and say to them, "Thanks, but I'm okay just as I am." Try devising a simple mantra to remind yourself that you are perfect just as you are and whatever you are tomorrow will also be perfect. (Example: "I have enough; I am enough.") Try it, and keep trying until you can believe it.*

Chapter 23:

Gratitude Is a Companion to Kindness

"If the only prayer you ever say in your entire life is thank you, it will be enough." (Meister Eckhart)

Many countries and cultures have holidays devoted to gratitude. Americans and Canadians celebrate Thanksgiving—though not on the same dates. It is an opportunity for us to pause and acknowledge our countries' heritage and all we—collectively and individually—have to be thankful for. Ideally, we should be doing this every day of our lives, but sometimes business and busyness crowd out gratitude.

Throughout my year of living kindly, I noticed over and over that kindness and gratitude go hand in hand and augment one another. This is never more evident to me as when I spend time in nature. Whether I'm hiking, relaxing on my deck with its view of the Cascade Mountains, or strolling my neighborhood, I often feel my heart opening to the nature around me—the flight and song of birds, the vast variety of trees and the way they change with the seasons, the surge of the creek in winter and its lazy amble in summer, the deer that visit our yard to nibble on the fallen apples. These things make me want to give back to the earth or to my community.

I was attending a weekend conference in Pittsburgh during my year of living kindly. It was late May, and the weather was glorious. I had a free afternoon, so I walked to a nearby park and sat on a bench with a book. I divided my time between reading and appreciating the sights around me. The park was like a living organism—children playing on the lawn, couples strolling hand in hand, squirrels, dogs, flowers, and endless varieties of trees and birds. I remember feeling the overwhelming sense of how blessed I was to be able to experience it all—the park, the conference, the travel, the people I was meeting, and the ideas I was encountering. Gratitude filled every pore. After a while, I walked to a local restaurant and ordered lunch. From my seat, I could still see the activity of the park and the bustle of Pittsburgh's busy streets. I asked the waitress to box up my fruit salad and the remaining half of my sandwich, thinking they would make a fine dinner. Walking back toward my hotel, I felt the fullness of my life and the amazing privilege of when, where, and how I am living. A block or so from my hotel, I noticed an elderly man slumped in a wheelchair. At his side was a can with a few coins in it and a small cardboard sign with lettering that said, "Please Help."

I stopped and greeted him. Then I said, "I have a half a turkey sandwich here and some fruit salad. Would you like them?"

His eyes widened and he said, "I surely would." I handed the restaurant bag to him and reached into my purse for a couple of dollars, which I also handed him. We talked for a minute or two, and I noticed how his eyes held a lively twinkle. When I resumed my walk toward my hotel, I felt even lighter and happier than I had before. My brief interaction with the man had felt good. While I'm sure he appreciated the sandwich and the few dollars I handed him, I sensed that even more, he appreciated *being seen*. He was used to people averting their eyes, ignoring him as they quickly walked by, even occasionally dropping some change or a couple of dollars into his can but then rushing off without a word. The gratitude I had been feeling opened me to extending a kindness and offering not just the gift of food or money, but the gift of my genuine attention. There was no question in my mind, though, that I had received the greater gift that afternoon.

I saw that when I am in touch with my gratitude, kindness flows naturally and effortlessly. If kindness feels hard to summon, I've learned that taking a moment to appreciate my surroundings, my friends and loved ones, or little things that fill me with delight, inspires a surge of kindness.

I've come to see that there are many ways that kindness and gratitude together produce almost alchemical results.

Slowing Down

Both gratitude and kindness ask us to slow down. Slowing down isn't always easy in our overscheduled and overactive lives. I often feel like I'm rushing from one deadline to the next, one obligation to the next, ruled by a lengthy to-do list. But slowing down is essential if we are to notice and appreciate the sunrise, the crocuses bursting forth, the birds circling overhead like ice-skaters with wings. And slowing down is essential if we are to notice the smile on the cashier's face, the door held open for us, or the myriad opportunities before us each day to extend our own kindnesses.

An Open Heart

When I experience gratitude, my heart feels open. It is a feeling of abundance and sufficiency. *This is all I need.* It is also a feeling of presence—what happened five minutes ago doesn't matter, and what will happen five minutes from now doesn't matter. I am in the moment.

Likewise, the experience of kindness—whether given, received, or even just witnessed—opens my heart and allows me to feel fully present in the moment. For that brief moment, kindness is all that matters. It reminds me of one of my very favorite quotes, by Henry James: "Three things in human life are important. The first is to be kind; the second is to be kind; and the third is to be kind."

As we saw in Chapter 22, abundance is also a companion of kindness. If we believe we *are* enough, we can easily believe we *have* enough. Both of these beliefs help us to reserve judgment and extend kindness. And that sense of abundance, whether related to gratitude or kindness—or most likely, both—inspires us to be generous with our time, our words, our deeds, and our resources.

Negative Emotions

I've found that it's difficult to be angry or fearful when one experiences gratitude. If my heart is grateful, I feel no need to summon ire if I am cut off in traffic or spoken to harshly. I'm less likely to be frightened by a new or daunting situation. Perhaps there's simply no space for these emotions when I am filled with gratitude, or maybe gratitude has a way of neutralizing the effects of these negative emotions.

This belief is often challenged when I hear about the most recent terrorist attack or the latest mass shooting. Those events spawn fear and anger, not just in the people directly affected, but in people all over the world. While there may also be gratitude that one's family and friends were spared, and gratitude for the outpouring of support for the victims, can gratitude completely rout the fear and anger? I think not. But maybe there can be moments when gratitude at least overrides fear and lets us see that there is much to appreciate, even in the midst of terror attacks, natural disasters, or personal catastrophe. Maybe it's gratitude that helps us recover from the worst things that can befall us.

Service to the Planet

When we are grateful for something, our instinct is to protect and defend it. If we stand in awe at the edge of the ocean, or if we marvel at the canopy of trees above us as we hike through the nearby hills, our natural desire is to shield them from harm, to assure that they will always be there for us and for future generations to appreciate. Our gratitude puts us in service to life—what could be more important?

Kindness, too, places us in service to life. We feel a physical connection to our surroundings and to the people around us when we engage in kind acts. Both the acts and the sense of connection are our acknowledgment that the ultimate kindness is to honor the earth and our fellow inhabitants—human and otherwise. A healthy planet and sustainable practices are the kindest gifts we can offer one another and the generations that follow us.

Gratitude Practices

It's lovely if gratitude comes to us frequently and effortlessly, but that is not always the case. Gratitude, like kindness, tennis, or piano-playing, is strengthened with practice. The more we do it, the more we experience it, and the better we become at expressing it. If you do an online search for "gratitude practices" you will find countless suggestions, from daily meditation, to keeping a gratitude journal, to prayer. I try to spend a few moments each morning before I get up thinking about the things I have to be grateful for. Another creative approach is to create "trigger" occasions that you use to establish a habit of gratitude. For example, every time you stop at a red light, use the moment to think of something you're grateful for.

There's another splendid gratitude practice that I love and practice occasionally. Physician and teacher Dr. Rachel Naomi Remen teaches this exercise[1] that she learned from anthropologist Angeles Arrien. It's simple and takes very little time. Here's all you do:

At the end of each day, sit down for a few minutes and answer these questions:

- What surprised me today?
- What moved or touched me today?
- What inspired me today?

Your answers can be just a few words. What you're trying to do is summon the memory of things that moved you.

As Dr. Remen describes: "The most interesting thing happens, then. Often people are surprised eight or nine hours after something happens when they look back on it deliberately. But [by doing this exercise] that gap shortens until eventually they are able to see in the very moment what surprises them, what touches them, and what inspires them. And then everything changes. The world has not changed, but they have begun to be able to see the world, and they can communicate that experience. . . . It changes everything. It's a question of paying attention."

It's true. At first this is difficult. You may come up blank day after day. *"Nothing surprised me,"* or *"Nothing inspired me."* But if you keep searching, you will think of something. *Oh, yes, I was touched when I saw those children playing in the park.* And just as Dr. Remen says, with practice you begin to notice things that touch or surprise or inspire you in the moment they happen. That creates an enduring state of gratitude—not to mention presence.

One of the greatest gifts we can give ourselves is taking the time to think about what we are grateful for—both the obvious and the small, hidden, even quirky things that enrich life. Daily recognition of the multitude of big and little things we have to be grateful for is a wonderful way to live in perpetual thanksgiving.

Kindness in Action: *Make an effort to say "thank you" more often in your daily interactions, and when you say it, mean it. If you don't already have one, think about a daily gratitude practice that will work for you—a gratitude journal, a few moments of reflection, a trigger activity, perhaps Rachel Remen's simple exercise—then try it for three weeks. Notice whether it changes your awareness of how many things there are in your life to be grateful for. Notice also if it makes you more aware of kindness—your own and others'. If you find yourself in a situation that may provoke anger or fear, try summoning gratitude to counteract their effects. Talk about gratitude with your family—perhaps make it a game at the dinner table, or when you're on a long drive, to name all the things you have to be grateful for.*

Chapter 24:

Kindness and Generosity:

It's Not All about Money

"Generosity brings happiness at every stage of its expression. We experience joy in forming the intention to be generous. We experience joy in the actual act of giving something. And we experience joy in remembering the fact that we have given."
(Gautama Buddha)

We've talked about the connection between kindness and a sense of abundance. The logical next step, when one's view of the world is of abundance rather than scarcity, is to express that abundance through generosity.

I have been blessed to be the recipient of so much generosity throughout my life—from my friends, my nonprofit clients and professional colleagues, my family, and even strangers. Their generosity is expressed through the wisdom they so willingly share, through their time, their thoughtful actions, and their kind words and understanding—even when I am not behaving at my best.

When we think of generosity, our first thoughts are likely of material gifts or donations of cash. Of course, these are elemental expressions of generosity, but they aren't our only gifts.

The Three Ts

There's an adage in the nonprofit world that board members need to be willing to give the three Ts: Time, Talent, and Treasure. **Treasure** is usually interpreted in monetary terms—especially for charitable and philanthropic organizations. If board members won't donate to the cause, it's hard to convince others to do so. Hence, grant applications will often ask if 100 percent of the board has made a donation to the organization. Boards with high rollers can usually easily answer yes, but if members of the board are part of the constituency the organization serves, there may be some who have little to spare in the treasure department. That's why grant applications don't ask how much board members have donated, only if they have. A $10 donation from someone who may have to skip a meal to make that donation is just as important—perhaps more so—as the $50,000 donation from a corporate CEO.

Being generous with our **talent** asks only that we are willing to share what we do best, whether that's fund-raising, marketing, budgeting, schmoozing, or baking cupcakes. Each of us has unique talents, and part of the job of being human is recognizing them and sharing them where they are most needed.

Generosity of **time** is an essential element in nonprofits and elsewhere. We are often so pressed for time, so overscheduled, that we blow off opportunities to extend kindness. Or maybe we don't even see them in our rush to meet so many deadlines. Generosity with our time when time is limited can be a kindness beyond measure—especially if we are able to give without conveying to the recipient our stress or our inconvenience.

Other Ways to Be Generous

Beyond the three Ts, there are a multitude of other ways we can be generous:

We can be generous in deed: It can be as simple as holding a door for someone, helping to carry a heavy load, or offering a hand. It might be bringing freshly made soup to a neighbor or washing someone else's dirty dishes without grousing. There are so many generous deeds we can offer—big and small—and mostly it's a matter of training our eyes to look for them.

We can be generous of word: It doesn't take much to make someone's day with a kind word. Mark Twain famously said, "I can live for two months on a good compliment." Of course, he is also reported to have said, "I have been complimented many times and they always embarrass me; I always feel they have not said enough." Both quotes show how powerful a sincerely expressed compliment can be. And the wonderful thing is that it's easy! We can compliment someone on the great service they provided, or the astuteness of an observation, a well-written report, or how their smile brightens a room. All we have to do is pay attention. Kind words can be spoken or written, and their impact can last a lifetime. I can still recall with pleasure kind words spoken decades ago, and I keep a file of notes and cards that I have treasured for years because of their heart-touching sentiments. Looking at them always buoys me.

We can be generous of spirit: The Buddhist practice of *metta*, often translated as "lovingkindness," teaches practitioners to repeat phrases—aimed first at oneself, then loved ones, then acquaintances and strangers, and finally even to adversaries. The phrases express a wish for happiness, for safety, peace, freedom from pain, and so forth. In offering *metta* to people with whom we share conflict or difficulties, people who have hurt or angered us, we are, says Buddhist teacher Sharon Salzberg[1], "recognizing our essential interconnectedness." Salzberg notes that in offering *metta* to a difficult person, we are not condoning bad or hurtful actions. "Instead, we are looking deeply into our hearts and discovering a capacity for lovingkindness that is not dependent on circumstances and personalities." We are expressing generosity not only to others but to ourselves. That capacity for compassion is our gift to the world.

If we can give nothing else, let us at least *give the benefit of the doubt*. This is easier to do with family and friends than with mere acquaintances and strangers. If a friend or loved one says something that we find hurtful, it's usually easy to excuse: "I'm sure that wasn't how she meant it," or "I know he's been under a lot of pressure; he didn't really mean it." Why can't we offer that same understanding to strangers when they say or do something questionable or hurtful? Instead, we generally ascribe the worst motives and label them jerks.

In our office, and on nonprofit boards I work with, we continually remind ourselves to "assume one another's good intent." A simple statement, but it is enormously powerful. If I could, I'd have that phrase printed at the top of every meeting agenda and posted on the wall of every room where people gather. It all comes down to the simple generosity of giving the benefit of the doubt to everyone we encounter.

Generosity isn't just something we do for someone else. When I choose to act generously, the greatest beneficiary is always myself. There is no better expression of the abundance in my life, nor of the confidence that I not only have enough, I *am* enough. Giving creates a joyful sense of oneness with my world and my fellow creatures.

Kindness in Action: *Think about when you've given your three Ts, your treasure, your talent, or your time. How did it feel? Is there someone who could be helped by one of your Ts today? What are some of your talents? Perhaps you're taking them for granted and don't recognize their worth. They may be business proficiencies, social skills, or creative abilities that you undervalue. Take a moment to recognize all that you have to offer. Look for a way, today, that you can be generous of word—a genuine compliment that you can express, or perhaps a note of appreciation that might make someone's day—don't let the day go by without giving that gift. It will please you as much as it does the recipient. And if you don't already keep a file of notes, cards, emails, and such in which people have told you how wonderful you are and how much they appreciate you, start one today. It's a great place to visit whenever you need a reminder of the difference you are making on the earth.*

Chapter 25:

Pay Attention:

Kindness Requires Presence

"Tell me what you pay attention to, and I will tell you who you are." (José Ortega y Gasset)

Remember how annoying it was as a child or adolescent to hear teachers repeatedly admonish their students to "Pay attention"? Sometimes it was code for "This will be on the test." Other times, it was said over and over because the teacher had lost the students' interest, and instructing them to pay attention was probably easier than exploring new ways of making geometry or eighteenth-century European history exciting.

All these years later, I keep a little slip of paper bearing the words "Pay Attention" taped next to my desk. I think it's one of the secrets to a good life and an essential requirement for living a kind life.

If we are unaware of what's going on around us, it's so easy to miss opportunities to be kind. It might be something simple like holding a door for a stranger, making eye contact and smiling, or offering to help someone who is struggling with heavy packages. Or it may not be so simple—it might be recognizing despair on a friend's face and taking time to listen to her story, or thinking about just the right words to say to help a child deal with disappointment or rejection. If we're oblivious, we miss all these instances where we might make a difference.

Opportunities to extend kindness are all around us, but they're also easy to miss if we aren't paying attention. And these days we're often so distracted by technology that we lose awareness of what is going on right in front of us.

Choosing Presence

Meetings are a major component of my profession: educational seminars, conferences, board meetings, committee meetings, breakfast/lunch/dinner meetings. It's how we learn, how we network, how we accomplish the business of our nonprofit organization clients.

It used to be that during breaks at meetings and conferences, people would help themselves to a cup of coffee and chat with others attending the meeting. Now, people still grab the coffee, but then they stand in solitude at a distance of about four feet from one another and they check email or their social media, they text or surf the net. They don't connect with other people in the room. I've had people admit to me that sometimes they check for nonexistent emails because it's what everyone else is doing, and they feel self-conscious just standing there with no one to talk to. I've done it myself.

That person-to-person networking of days gone by was often as valuable as the formal education at the meetings. It's where practical, informal learning took place, not to mention cultivating business connections and making friends. And for younger people just entering professional life, it was often where they could hone their social skills, skills essential to advancement. Can we find a balance between staying connected electronically and connecting at a human level? I would happily forego some time with my technology to restore some old-fashioned face-to-face interaction.

I think we've lost sight of both our capacity and our obligation to set boundaries. We've let the devices rule us, when it should be the other way around.

At the park near our house, I see parents absorbed in their smartphones, ignoring their children's exuberant cartwheels or triumphant heights on the swings. I wonder whose loss is greater here. At the symphony recently, I saw the glow of many handheld devices—their operators oblivious to the magnificence of a Sibelius concerto. What are we missing when we choose not to be fully present in our lives?

I've been told that my notions are old-fashioned. I've even been called an "old fogey" for suggesting that we don't always need to be connected to our devices. "Technology is the future," I'm told. "If you're not connected, you're lagging behind." I'll concede that this is a decision each of us needs to make for ourselves.

When I lead groups in strategic planning, I remind them that everything they say "yes" to means there is something else they must say "no" to—so they need to think hard about what is most important to them. It's the same for us as individuals: What are we saying "no" to as we say "yes" to perpetual connectivity?

Mindfulness Fosters Compassion

There is research from Jon Kabat-Zinn[1] and others that mindfulness cultivates compassion and altruism. Experiments[2] have shown that mindfulness training makes people more likely to recognize and help others—even strangers—in need. It's a matter of having our eyes open and seeing what's in front of us. If we're present for our lives—paying attention—we're going to recognize when our gifts are needed: a smile, a word of kindness, a proffered hand.

It's true for self-kindness, too. If we are aware and awake to our lives, we are more likely to recognize that we are tired and need to rest, or that we are stressed and need to pause. As we cultivate awareness of our own lives, we will be better able to recognize and respond to the needs of others. We can't live a life of kindness toward others if we are not kind to ourselves.

And it all begins with the simple act of choosing to be present, and choosing again and again what we will pay attention to.

 Kindness in Action: *Can you think of a time when you missed something wonderful (not necessarily big, but wonderful) because you were either oblivious or absorbed in your device or smartphone? Have you—like so many of us—all too often allowed the urgent to crowd out the important in your life? Are there boundaries you could set (and keep!) that would help you to stay present and aware throughout your day? Try it for just one day, and see what happens. Also for just a day, or a week, cultivate a practice of pausing to pay attention to what you're feeling. Do you need to rest, to eat, to breathe, or even to just have a few moments of quiet? Give yourself that gift, and see how it feels.*

Chapter 26:

Dancing with Understanding:

Two Steps Forward, One Step Back

"My religion is very simple. My religion is kindness."
(Dalai Lama)

We've talked about the power of the pause in guiding us to act kindly and recognize kindness as we are experiencing it. The all-important pause also has power when we're trying to learn something new. It allows us to assess, evaluate, question, and set new intentions. As we've seen, a pause is not an empty space—it's a choice-point. Let's pause again here and take an opportunity to reflect upon the last dozen chapters.

What are you thinking about kindness and how you have been experiencing it—as a receiver of kindness, a giver of kindness, and a witness of the kindness of others? Have you been able to put kindness into practice daily—even in what may seem like small ways to you? What is it about being kind that challenges you most? What people or circumstances have been the most trying? Are you noticing kindness more—in the people around you, the books or news you read, even your own ability to recognize when you need some TLC?

Are you noticing when you respond instantly to people or situations—and later wish you'd paused and thought a bit more about your reaction? And are you finding it easy to choose kindness and to recommit to it—knowing that it's sometimes hard, sometimes misunderstood, and sometimes you will fall short?

Take a moment to think about the kindnesses you've extended and even to imagine the ripple effect they've had. You are actively creating a kinder world. Congratulations! Set some intentions for the days and weeks ahead. Where would you most like to see more kindness in your life, and where can you more readily embrace kindness? Here are some ideas:

- Can you admit when your own fear—of embarrassment, rejection, or vulnerability—makes you impolite or prone to be snappish?
- Can you reframe your attitude toward time so you see kindness as a priority and not something that strains your patience or disrupts your schedule?
- If you extend a kindness and it is rejected, can you acknowledge your embarrassment or hurt feelings and accept that you did your best, not taking the rejection personally?
- Do you look for ways to be kind to yourself—a nature walk, a nap, an hour with a good book, a bubble bath, or some music you can shake your booty to?
- Are you learning to accept compliments and kindnesses with grace, thus giving back to the giver?
- Are you looking for ways you can extend micro-kindnesses, realizing that each small gesture and each tiny, noticeable thing ultimately contributes to a positive world?
- Are you better able to overcome those times when you feel "less than"—when the media, friends, family members, or even yourself, send you messages that you should be smarter, prettier, thinner, more successful . . . or otherwise different from

what you are? Have you been able to tune out those voices and appreciate what you are and what you have and know it is enough?

- Have you experienced the connection between gratitude and kindness? Do you make time for gratitude every day—through a gratitude practice, a few moments of reflection, or more generous (and genuine) use of the phrase "thank you"?

- Have you taken some time to assess your "three Ts"? Even if you don't have *treasure* to spare to express your generosity, what special *talents* can you offer, and where can you give the gift of your *time*?

- Have you been able to express your generosity through simple deeds, kind and compassionate words, or offering the benefit of the doubt where once you might have judged harshly?

- Have you taken some time to think about what you want to pay attention to, and choices you may sometimes need to make to live a "kindful" life?

- If there are kids in your life, do you remember to have conversations with them about kindness and related values, such as gratitude, generosity, and happiness? Remember to listen to their observations and experiences. Children can be powerful little ambassadors for kindness.

- Revisit some of our earlier kindness conversations: Are you less judgy? Can you make time for kindness without stressing? Can you extend kindness to people whose behavior bewilders you? Have you stopped keeping score in your relationships?

Take a few moments to appreciate all the kindness you have added to the world. It has made a difference even if you haven't seen it. As you celebrate kindness as your new superpower, know that it will become ever stronger and more transformative as you continue to use it!

PART THREE:

The Season
of Choosing

I. The Tools of Kindness

Chapter 27:

A Life of Kindness Requires Courage

"Life shrinks or expands in proportion to one's courage."
(Anaïs Nin)

It takes courage to stand up to a schoolyard bully, or to make friends with a child whom others have ostracized. It takes courage to speak out against powerful people who incite bigotry or injustice, and it takes courage to offer words of consolation when you simply don't know what to say.

As I ventured through my year of living kindly, I was struck repeatedly by how often it takes courage to be kind. Extending kindness to others—and even to ourselves—risks judgment, rejection, or going against prevailing winds. Sometimes it means we make ourselves vulnerable or chance looking foolish. Courage is required if we are to overcome all of those risks. As Wayne Muller says, "A kind life . . . is fundamentally a life of courage."

Many of us have a limited view of what courage is. We may perceive it as the quality we summon when faced with danger or extreme risk. It's what we need to jump out of a plane, run into a burning building, or face a life-threatening illness. Undoubtedly, those circumstances do call for courage, but there's another kind of courage that an authentic life asks of us.

Courage expert Sandra Ford Walston[1] differentiates split-second heroism from everyday courage. While the former may be a spontaneous reaction to traumatic events or perilous circumstances, the latter is more subtle, yet no less important. "Sometimes small acts require great courage," says Walston. "We see it in the workplace when one has the courage to ask for the long overdue raise, or take the risk to leave a job without another in place, or confront a workplace bully. Elsewhere in our lives, one may demonstrate courage when summoning the strength to end a relationship, or the conviction to enter one. For women, especially, learning to ask for what you want is often an act of courage."

Walston further explains that the word "courage" originates from the Old French *corage*, meaning "heart and spirit." This, she says, "takes us beyond the narrow definition of bravery in the face of danger to encompass mental or moral strength."

There are times when kind actions make us vulnerable, or when our kindness is rejected or even ridiculed. Sometimes kindness means choosing not to be indifferent or acting contrary to what is expected of us. Sometimes it means speaking up—and other times, remaining silent. Courage is required if we are to overcome all those risks and extend the kindness that comes from our most authentic self.

Such courage requires that we pay attention. Mindfulness is an essential element of courage, just as it is of kindness. It's so easy to miss opportunities to be courageous, or to fail to recognize when we have acted courageously.

Kindness and courage intersect when we stand up for someone who is being bullied, or when we speak out against injustice, or when we risk ridicule or rejection to do what we believe to be the kind thing. Sometimes it takes courage to ask for what we want, to admit we are wrong, or to change the tone of a conversation. Says Walston, "If I am centered in my courage, I will naturally display kindness." This, she says, is "where courage meets grace."

For me, the courage kindness required became evident in small things. As I found and used my voice more often, it became easier to speak up on someone's behalf or to say words of comfort. It became easier to engage with a stranger and offer help.

I think we so often equate courage with heroic deeds and superhuman exploits that we don't recognize the importance of small, everyday courageous actions. Just as there are no small acts of kindness, I don't think there are insignificant acts of courage. It takes courage to be the first person to speak out in a meeting if someone says something intolerant or insensitive. It takes courage to take the hand of a friend who is dying or grieving and offer genuine comfort, even when we have no words. It takes courage to admit we are lost, hurting, and in need of help to get through a difficult time.

Sometimes, it takes courage to tell the truth—to ourselves and to others—to reveal that we're not as smart, successful, or interesting as we pretend to be. But exercising that courage is the ultimate kindness—it gives us permission to be authentic and exhibits the trust that others will accept and respect us for who we really are. Choosing kindness over fear is an act of extreme courage—even if no one else ever knows or sees what we did.

Committing to a life of kindness—knowing there will be some who dismiss it as weak or insignificant—is a true act of courage. Additionally, the vulnerability of allowing ourselves to be seen as weak, imperfect, or flawed requires similar courage. It takes courage to live with integrity every day.

Courage and kindness share another quality: they are both strengthened with practice.

Kindness in Action: *Take some time to think about where courage shows up in your life and where courage and kindness have intersected. Recognize all the times you've been both courageous and kind. If you're a parent, do your children see your courage when you go out of your way to extend kindness? Talk with them about how kindness sometimes requires courage, and how both of those qualities prepare them for a life of integrity. Is there a kind action that you have avoided out of fear? Strategize how you will claim your courage and extend kindness when the opportunity next arises.*

Chapter 28:

Kindness and Curiosity

"Curiosity is the single most important attribute with which humans are born. More than a simple desire to discover or know things, curiosity is a powerful tool, like a scalpel or a searchlight. Curiosity changes us. It is also a way to effect change, perhaps even on a global level." (Loren Rhoads)

I was surprised when I first heard kindness equated with curiosity. The connection wasn't obvious to me, but it made *me* curious. I've always thought curiosity was an important quality to have if one wanted a rich and insightful life, and I am only too happy to welcome the connection between these two powerful forces.

In an article entitled "Kindness and Curiosity in Coaching,"[1] business consultant and executive coach Ruth Henderson described how her mother would suggest a kind explanation for other people's behavior. After being cut off by a speeder, Ruth's mom would speculate, "Maybe his wife's having a baby, and he's trying to get to the hospital."

Later, when Ruth was a business professional, her own coach encouraged her to approach difficult or frustrating situations with an inquisitive mind. She told Ruth, "Kindness and curiosity leave no room for anger and resentment."

I think it's true. If I ponder a work situation where a colleague did something that seemed terribly inappropriate, or a client blew up and offended everyone within earshot, it's easy to get angry or judge that person harshly. But if I tap into my curiosity first, I have a very different response. What made that colleague choose to act inappropriately? Was she acting out of fear? Was there a misunderstanding? Did she somehow not realize the nature of her action? Is something else going on in her life that I'm not aware of?

And what made that client blow up? Fear is often behind many such outbursts—what might he be afraid of? Or maybe he's not feeling appreciated, or perhaps there's a personal calamity in his life that has stressed him to his limits? What don't I know that might explain his behavior?

As soon as I yield to curiosity and allow for the possibility that there may be something going on that is beyond my awareness, I can replace my reflex response of anger or distaste with a desire to understand and even a desire to help. Curiosity leads to kindness.

Curiosity and Discipline

In an article[2] that appeared in the *Harvard Business Review*—one that I think should be required reading for anyone who manages or supervises other people, or who wants to—Stanford University research psychologist Emma Seppälä, PhD, describes how compassion and curiosity are more effective than frustration and reprimand in responding to an underperforming employee or one who has made a serious mistake.

Traditional, authoritarian management approaches tend to focus on reprimanding, criticizing, even frightening the employee—the rationale being that fear and embarrassment might show the individual the error of his ways. He'll change in order to avoid another scolding. Instead, the research reveals, it serves mostly to erode loyalty and trust, and to impede creativity and innovation.

A more effective response to an employee's error or underperformance is to first get our own emotions in control, and then view the situation from the employee's eyes. Here's where curiosity comes into play. What caused the mistake, or what might be the reason for the poor performance? What is the employee feeling about the error that he made? Chances are he is horrified, embarrassed, and frightened. A kind response—this doesn't mean overlooking the error, but compassionately using it as a teaching or coaching opportunity—will instill loyalty, trust, and even devotion. It will also be far more effective than reprimand or punishment in helping the employee avoid such mistakes in the future.

The loyalty engendered by the kind response extends beyond the particular employee you may be dealing with. As Seppälä notes, "If you are more compassionate to your employee, not only will he or she be more loyal to you, but anyone else who has witnessed your behavior may also experience elevation and feel more devoted to you." As we've seen elsewhere, merely witnessing kindness directed toward others increases our own emotional well-being.

It makes sense. Everyone makes mistakes, and if our employees see their boss or manager respond kindly to a coworker's blunder, they can feel secure in the knowledge that when they make a mistake, the response is likely to be similarly compassionate. This fosters a culture of safety, one that encourages innovation, creativity, productivity, and loyalty—these are the qualities that the best and the brightest are seeking for their career homes.

Whoever said "Curiosity killed the cat" had it wrong. Curiosity is one of the most beneficial qualities we can cultivate. Combine it with kindness, and magic happens!

Kindness in Action: *Next time you are the recipient of apparent rudeness or unkindness, make an effort to engage your curiosity before unleashing your ire or frustration. Open your mind to the possibility that there may be another explanation for that person's behavior, and that it was not intentionally directed at you. Try to come up with a plausible explanation and—even if you're pretty certain the behavior resulted from malice or indifference—give the benefit of the doubt. If doing that makes you feel weak or exploited, explore whether that is something you can accept in the service of kindness. If the answer is "no," that's perfectly okay. Just own whatever you're feeling, and be aware of what you would like to feel.*

*Think about the best and worst bosses you ever had. What made them that way? Did one boss instantly react and berate you or someone else if a mistake was made? Did another take the time to explore what happened and understand, and help you find a way to fix the problem and prevent it from happening again? If you're in a management or supervisory position, which way do you usually react? Consider creating a simple trigger reminder—perhaps just a big **?**—to remind you to approach life with healthy curiosity.*

Chapter 29:

Kindness and Vulnerability

"A gift is like a seed; it is not an impressive thing. It is what can grow from the seed that is impressive. If we wait until our seed becomes a tree before we offer it, we will wait and wait, and the seed will die from lack of planting. . . . The miracle is not just the gift; the miracle is in the offering, for if we do not offer, who will?" (Wayne Muller)

In high-tech parlance, vulnerability refers to a weakness or flaw that allows an attacker to access a computer without the owner's permission. In human terms, vulnerability describes our susceptibility to being wounded or injured, and also the state of being exposed—to danger, illness, or criticism. For many of us, vulnerability implies weakness. It is something to be avoided.

But is it? Vulnerability may be our way of opening ourselves to the world, and trusting that it is not against us. It may be our way of embracing mystery and not pushing the unknown or the unseen away from us. It may be the truest way of saying "yes" to our lives.

In a relationship, we may be vulnerable when we are first to say "I love you," or when we admit we don't know something, or that we need help. Our comfort and security are threatened by the "power" we believe we have given the other person. Will he say he loves me back? Will she take advantage of my weakness if I ask for help? Yes, those fears are real. But another way to look at them is to recognize the strength they reveal and to take ownership of that strength. There is no shame in loving, even if the other person doesn't love me back. There is no shame in asking for help, even if it isn't given. The weakness is in burying our feelings or denying our need.

Dr. Brené Brown, research professor at the University of Houston, describes how vulnerability is a trait that wholehearted people share. As she explains in a remarkable TED Talk[1] and in her audiobook *The Power of Vulnerability: Teachings on Authenticity, Connection, and Courage*[2], vulnerability is the courage to be imperfect, to do something where there are no guarantees, and to let go of who we think we should be in order to be what we really are. With this willingness, we "allow ourselves to be seen," with all our imperfections, in order to fully embrace our lives. Dr. Brown further explains that many of us erroneously believe that we can selectively numb our emotions; that we can stifle grief, shame, fear, and disappointment while fully retaining our joy, gratitude, and happiness. It doesn't work that way. If we suppress the negative emotions, we do the same to the positive ones. Accepting our vulnerability and living wholeheartedly means understanding that the good, the bad, and even the ugly are what make us authentic and beautiful. That place of vulnerability, she says, is the birthplace of joy, creativity, belonging, and love.

Whether we're committing to love, or art, or business, or kindness, we must have the courage to do it wholeheartedly, in spite of the fact that we know there will always be those who find us lacking. Knowing this is incredibly freeing! We can't please everyone. Not ever. So we need to stop trying and focus instead on being who we are meant to be.

The more I think about it, the more deeply I see the connection between kindness and vulnerability. I've talked before about the difference between being kind and being nice. *Nice* does not require me to be vulnerable. I can be nice without risk, and without exposing too much of myself. I can be nice without making a connection, or without really caring whether or not you benefit from the encounter. Nice, while pleasant, doesn't require sincerity or commitment. When I'm nice, I remain safe, guarded from exposure.

Kind is very different. Kind means connecting; it means being aware and intentional about the impact my words and actions have; it means expending energy and effort, and caring about the outcome. It means exposing my truest self in all my imperfections. It also means suspending judgments and accepting people as they are. Kind can be messy, and it may take me to places where I am awkward, clumsy, and tongue-tied. Kindness requires me to take risks. In short, kindness requires me to be vulnerable.

Since making a commitment to living kindly, I have tried to replace *nice* with *kind*. The distinction may not have been noticeable to anyone but me. But my noticing it is really all that matters. Whether acknowledging someone's assistance, explaining a new process, or giving a couple of dollars to someone in need, I try to make a connection, even if it's only fleeting. Taking the time to make eye contact, exchange a few words, and convey that I *see* a person and recognize their value—these small actions convey our shared humanity and our shared vulnerability. It feels good.

My upbringing—and I suspect I am not alone in this—was one where I was encouraged to be smart. Grades were important to my parents, and I was rewarded for good ones. Poor grades (that is, anything less than an A) were a disappointment, and I dreaded the thought of disappointing my parents. Being smart and being right became important to my identity. School and career generally reinforced the importance of those qualities. There came a point, though, when I started to see that I wasn't always smart, and I certainly wasn't always right. At first, this felt threatening. If I admit how little I know about this subject or this new technology, will people assume

I'm ignorant? Will I be giving up some imaginary advantage I have? It took both courage and a willingness to be vulnerable to start saying, "I don't understand," or "Please show me how this works." It took even more to ask to be shown again when the first lesson didn't "take."

Rather than judging me harshly, I saw that people welcomed my questions. They appreciated the opportunity to share knowledge in areas where they excelled. I learned to ask questions that deepened my understanding. I breathed a sigh of relief that I was not expected to know everything, understand everything, or always be right. I didn't have to fake knowledge I didn't have. I was surrounded by smart people and, in aggregate, we were very, very smart. The other thing I saw when I was willing to show my vulnerability and admit my ignorance or inexperience was that others seemed more comfortable coming to me to either ask my help or admit when they needed help. I think it must be very lonely to feel you must always have the answers or be the smartest person in the room.

There is even a vulnerability to writing or speaking about kindness, and inviting people to read or hear my thoughts. Sharing my deepest thoughts—what matters most to me— opens me to their judgment, perhaps to criticism. Beyond that, am I saying too much about myself? Too little? Am I pontificating (oh, I hope not!)? Has it all been said before and said better? Am I missing the point entirely?

If I allow myself to be vulnerable, the answer is that *it doesn't matter.* As Brené Brown eloquently explains[3], connection is why we're all here, sharing this planet, and it's what gives meaning and purpose to our lives. To make that deep connection, *we have to allow ourselves to be seen.* That means having the courage to be imperfect, to expose our flaws, and the willingness to be vulnerable.

You may feel awkward, exposed, or uncomfortable when you first start heeding the call to kindness. Good! That means you've tapped into your vulnerability. Embrace it, and keep allowing your kindness to grow.

Living our most authentic life, whatever that means to

each of us, requires that we let go of our shield and lower our guard, and that we embrace our flaws and our vulnerability. For me—and perhaps for you—it's choosing kindness. It's scary, but the rewards of living an authentic life are beyond measure.

__Kindness in Action:__ Can you think of a time when you felt vulnerable? Recall the situation and your response. Did you back away to "safety"? Or did you forge ahead? Either way, try to imagine the outcome of the situation had you done the opposite of what you did. Maybe it feels better, or maybe worse, but can you feel the strength of your response when you accept your vulnerability? Think about the you that most people see: Is that person authentic and real, or are you projecting only what you think they want to see, or what you feel safe allowing to be seen? What is your relationship to perfection? Do you strive for it, or do you recognize that perfection is a myth that keeps us from being the interesting, contradictory, and often messy human beings that we all are at our core? Are there messages you received as a child that no longer serve you but that you continue to hold onto? If you're a parent, do the messages your children receive encourage them to be authentic and vulnerable, or to strive for impossible perfection? If you haven't seen Brené Brown's TED Talk, make yourself a cup of tea and google it. It will be a very worthwhile twenty minutes!

Chapter 30:

Choosing to Be For or Against

"Kindness can become its own motive. We are made kind by being kind." (Eric Hoffer)

These days, when I read the newspaper or listen to the news, I find myself looking or listening for stories about kindness. I like to think that I'm developing a radar of sorts—an inner homing device that seeks and recognizes kindness. I'm a firm believer in the idea that we tend to see whatever it is we're looking for. If we spend our days looking for what's wrong, we will become skilled at finding what's broken, insufficient, or flawed. And if we look for what's good and right and hopeful, that's what we will find.

For many years, I've had pinned to my bulletin board an old Ashleigh Brilliant postcard that says, "If you look hard enough for what doesn't exist, eventually it may appear." Some time ago, a friend noticed it and asked me why that was on my wall, when all my other quotes and cartoons were so positive. I was baffled.

I told her, "But that *is* positive. It tells me to keep striving for what I believe in. Even if I can't yet see it, it's there waiting for me to find it. What do you think it means?"

Something quite different, it would seem. She told me, "If I think my husband is cheating on me, and I look hard enough, I'll find out it's true."

Well, I guess that is one way of looking at it. [Spoiler alert: that marriage didn't last much longer.]

To a large degree, I think we do make our own reality. I've known people who have had more than their share of loss, illness, and misfortunes, yet they maintain a positive outlook and still manage to find something good in every experience. They are a joy to be around.

I've also known people who see every loss and every mishap as proof that the world is against them and life's not fair. They enter every new experience with the expectation that they will be disappointed or somehow taken advantage of, and, more often than not, they prove themselves right. More of the same is pretty much all they expect of life, and that pervading gloom is what they convey to others. Spending time with these energy vampires can be unpleasant and exhausting.

I'm not advocating being a Pollyanna. Perpetual and mindless cheerfulness can be as tiresome as the persistent pessimist. But if our radar is focused like a heat-seeking missile on finding mistakes, slights, and shortcomings, then life is probably pretty bleak. It's the old glass-half-full or glass-half-empty conundrum, once again.

Each of us needs to choose how we want to see life. And we must choose what we stand for and when we will stand. I think of it as being an activist in my own life. It needn't mean chaining oneself to a tree or staging a sit-in on a busy street (or perhaps it might!), but it means in our own way standing up for what we believe. When we see unkindness, injustice, or prejudice, we speak or stand for kindness, justice, and inclusion. How we do that often makes the difference between living a life of stark negativity or one of fertile optimism.

Mother Teresa is reported to have said, "I was once asked why I don't participate in antiwar demonstrations. I said that I will never do that, but as soon as you have a pro-peace rally, I'll be there."

I was reminded of that quote when I read an article[1] in the *Seattle Times.* Columnist Jerry Large wrote about a woman in the small, semirural town of Snohomish, north of Seattle, who was being removed as a volunteer leader in Young Life, a well-established Christian organization for high school students. Pam Elliott's "crime" was participating with other mothers in making decorations for the Seattle Pride Parade, and posting the pictures on her Facebook page. She did it in support of a friend and the friend's gay son, and because she believes in equality for everyone.

"Love is love," Elliott said. "I am not a big activist. I'm supporting my friend. This is what we do for each other; we love each other's kids like our own."

The Young Life people gave her a choice. Ms. Elliott could continue her work as a volunteer leader—work that she loved—if she retracted her Facebook posting and stopped aligning herself with the gay rights movement. The choice she made was to continue to support her friend and her friend's son . . . and what she felt was right. I'm not comparing Pam Elliott with Mother Teresa, but, like Mother Teresa, Ms. Elliott chose to stand *for* something rather than *against* something else.

The more we choose positive over negative, good over bad, kindness over apathy, the closer we all move toward manifesting the world we want to live in, and want future generations to know without question.

That's what I look for when I read the news, and when I find it, it gives me hope.

Kindness in Action: *Do you approach most new experiences with a sense of dread or one of positive anticipation? Can you think of a time when a result or response was influenced by your outlook—positive or negative? Are there attitudes in your life that you could change just by wording them differently? Instead of disliking a belief, or circumstance, or behavior, could you instead focus on liking its opposite? Instead of condemning bigotry, for example, could you applaud inclusiveness? For the next few days, try paying attention to the point of view you bring to experiences and encounters, and think about whether that viewpoint in any way affects the outcome.*

II. Choosing Kindness

Chapter 31:

What Do You Want Your Legacy to Be?

"It is not the nature of the task, but its consecration, that is the vital thing." (Martin Buber)

In the preface to his book *The Road to Character*[1], David Brooks talks about the difference between "résumé virtues" and "eulogy virtues." Brooks describes the former as the skills and proficiencies you list on your résumé—those abilities that help you land a job and be successful in your profession. He describes eulogy virtues as the qualities that are likely to be mentioned at your funeral, "the ones that exist at the core of your being— whether you are kind, brave, honest, or faithful; what kind of relationships you formed." Brooks admits that for much of his life he gave priority to résumé qualities rather than eulogy ones.

Shortly after encountering Brooks's notion of eulogy virtues, I attended a memorial service for a neighbor who had died unexpectedly. Amidst the sadness, there was abundant laughter. Friends, family members, neighbors, and work colleagues stood up to tell stories of this man's generosity and his consideration. Stories of how he patiently taught his grandchildren to fish, of how he comforted the little ones when they were frightened, how he was the first to offer help to a neighbor, and how he could tell a story better than anybody. Despite the fact that he was an extremely accomplished and successful businessman, even his work colleagues stood to extol his sense of humor, his generosity—his big-heartedness. Nobody mentioned his technical skill or his financial success. As important as those things had been in his life, they weren't what he would be remembered for.

I don't suppose many of us want to think about our funerals, or what people are going to be saying about us as they stand somberly at the podium or nosh on Swedish meatballs and potato salad later. But it's probably a safe bet that they're not going to be talking about the wealth or possessions we accumulated. And they're not going to be lauding our knack with PowerPoint or Excel, or our ability to sell cars, write code, or design heating systems. And if perchance they do, it won't be about the skill itself, but about the heart and soul that we brought to that ability.

Maybe they'll talk about the passion we brought to our job, the humor, the patience, the integrity, the kindness. And separate from our jobs, they'll talk about the qualities that stood out to them. For each of us, those will be different and they may include courage, loyalty, reliability, devotion, compassion, commitment. Each friend and colleague will likely see us differently: to one we were a mentor, to another a buddy, and to yet another we were a sociable neighbor or a wisecracking cubicle mate. Each will recall different special qualities depending on the relationship and their own needs and interactions. Yet each of us probably has a few overarching qualities that others recognize as our legacy.

Even for those whose jobs contributed significantly to the community's, or perhaps the world's, well-being—doctor, statesman, author, scientist—it's not necessarily the skill or the accomplishment that will be cited, but the dedication and intentionality that accompanied that accomplishment. Equally important as the surgeon's skill with the scalpel is the compassion she brings to her patients and their families, and to her colleagues in the operating theater. And if the author who pens the greatest literary work of the twenty-first century is seen off the page as one of the biggest jerks of the century, too, he has earned—at best—hollow tributes.

It bears thinking about now if we want to leave behind us a legacy of friendship, or courage, or faith . . . or kindness. And if we want to face the end of our life with no regrets. As we cultivate our skills in order to achieve professional or creative success, we need also to cultivate the qualities of personal success, those that go beyond our technical or career proficiencies. Think about what values or virtues you want to don each morning when you rise, wear throughout your day, and tuck under your pillow when you sleep. Whether it's faith, kindness, integrity, friendship, courage, or all of the above, choose to live your eulogy every day.

 Kindness in Action: *Think about what your résumé virtues are and what your eulogy virtues are (or what you'd like them to be). Where do you focus most of your attention? If you were to die tomorrow, what would people be most likely to say or remember about you? What would you like to be remembered for? If that isn't how you're currently living your life, what could you do today to start living your most desired legacy? It's never too late to become who you were meant to be.*

Chapter 32:

Extending Kindness to All:

Kindness Isn't Selective or Conditional

"Being considerate of others will take your children further in life than any college degree." (Marian Wright Edelman)

As my year of living kindly got underway, I found that I was noticing more, not just about my own experiences of kindness—extending it and receiving it—but also observing how people interacted with one another. It wasn't always pretty. I overheard the receptionist in a medical office speak rudely to an elderly patient, unable to disguise her impatience with the man's inability to understand his copayment. Checking into a lovely resort hotel in San Diego, I listened uncomfortably as the desk clerk apologized to a dissatisfied guest that there were no rooms to upgrade her to; the woman turned away in anger, commenting loudly on what a mistake her secretary had made in reserving a room for her at this hotel. When it was my turn to check in, I made a point of telling the desk clerk how lovely the hotel was and how much I was looking forward to my stay. He smiled gratefully. It takes so little!

Sometimes people simply seem to be oblivious to opportunities to be kind, but other times—in business situations, on the streets, in shops—it seems as if people sometimes judge the importance of others before deciding how to treat them.

Years ago, there was a story[1] on the news here in Washington about an incident in the eastern part of our state. A man who had been working on refurbishing a building he owned took a break to cash a check at his bank, after which he asked to have his parking voucher validated. The teller took one look at his shabby clothes and told him that cashing a check was not a sufficient transaction to justify the sixty-cent validation. The customer asked to speak to the bank manager, who looked him up and down and also refused to validate parking. Both bank employees assumed he was indigent and spoke impolitely and dismissively to him. In response to the inhospitable treatment, the customer withdrew all his money—over a million dollars—and took it to another bank down the street.

As the story was repeated in different news media, the moral seemed to be "Don't judge a book by its cover," but that misses the point. It implies that if, indeed, he had been a vagrant, then it would have been okay to disrespect him. It's never okay to disrespect anyone. The deeper lesson of the story is that kindness isn't situational, and it isn't reserved for some people and not others.

There's an old adage that "A person who is kind to you but rude to the waiter is not a kind person." We've all seen it: some clueless person who treats a waiter, or a cashier, or a laborer as if they don't matter and are only on the planet to serve Mr. or Ms. Clueless.

And we've also witnessed the people who fall all over themselves to be agreeable when the individuals they are dealing with are wealthy, famous, or "important," but who look at the rest of us as if we are either invisible or something to be scraped off the bottom of a shoe.

There was an instance in my office when someone phoned me to promote his boss, a national speaker, as a presenter for our clients' conferences. He was flattering and friendly—he clearly wanted to do business with us and saw me as the key to that door. We had a pleasant conversation, and I told him to send me more information about his boss. When I hung up, our receptionist, Alison, came into my office to ask if he had been as rude to me as he had to her. He had bullied her and spoken to her as an underling; he had been pushy and disrespectful in his insistence that he *had* to speak with me—*now*. Quite the opposite of the differential treatment I received. Needless to say, we never hired his boss to work with any of our clients. I won't encourage bullies!

Robert Louis Stevenson famously said, "Sooner or later everyone sits down to a banquet of consequences." That's a lesson this fellow could use. The food at such a banquet is far more appetizing for those who consistently choose kindness.

Some people seem to think they only need to be nice to people who—in some way or another—can help them achieve their aims. Maybe it's advancing their career or making an advantageous introduction. Perhaps—like the bank teller— they make a judgment: *this is (or isn't) an important person, and I will treat them accordingly.*

Where do people learn that they don't have to be kind to the waiter, the receptionist, the service worker, or the homeless person? I suspect they learn from watching others—parents first, but then teachers, bosses, friends, strangers. Maybe they see it on television. Children mimic what they see, not always understanding why. Parents and teachers are wise to remember the Marian Wright Edelman quote that opened this chapter and teach children the enormous lifelong value of practicing kindness.

It's true that there are some people who don't see any value to being kind unless it can get them something. There are always going to be a few people who are—let's face it—bozos. But most of us aren't. We just need reminders occasionally that kindness begets further kindness, and that choosing kindness costs nothing.

True kindness isn't selective. A kind person doesn't pick and choose whom to be kind to.

Kindness in Action: *What are you noticing as you make your own commitment to kindness? Does it sometimes appear to be selective? Can you recall an instance where someone— perhaps yourself—was treated with more or less kindness or respect because of his or her position or appearance? If you find yourself making judgments about others, can you trace where you learned those judgments? Can you let them go? Make an effort to remember that every person you meet deserves kindness and respect.*

Chapter 33:

Oh, the Stories We Tell!

"The beginning of personal transformation is absurdly easy.
We have only to pay attention to the flow of attention itself."
(Marilyn Ferguson)

We learned in drivers' training that everyone has a blind spot, or **scotoma**. We can't help it. Because of the way the eye is constructed, there is a location in the eye that no light reaches, resulting in obstructed or flawed vision. We may never be aware of our blind spots, though, because we're really good at compensating—our brains are able to fill in the gap so the surrounding picture appears absolutely complete.

Beyond the physical level, we have blind spots on a psychological level, too, and our brains also attempt to explain the unknown data—with mixed results. We've all been there: when we lack information, our brains make up stories to fill in the gaps—often the stories are both erroneous and damaging.

Perhaps two coworkers, with whom you often lunch, head out at noon without asking if you'd like to join them. Bewildered, you make up a story: you offended Carrie when you said you didn't have time to check the figures on the budget she was working on, or you ticked off Erika by not stopping to chat when you came in this morning. They probably think you're mad at them, and now they're mad at you. They're at lunch talking about you and saying nasty things about you.

By the time they return from lunch thirty minutes later, you've woven such a tale of perfidy that you've convinced yourself they no longer want to be your friend and nobody else in the office wants to be either. Why should they, after all? You're a terrible, horrible, very bad person!

When Carrie and Erika walk in, carrying fast-food takeout bags, you learn that Erika dropped her car off for servicing and Carrie followed to pick her up and drive her back to the office. As they'd feared, it took so long that they only had time to stop for some mediocre takeout, which they'll now have to eat at their desks.

The story you constructed was entirely false—nobody was mad, nobody was offended, nobody was saying terrible things about you behind your back, and you are not a terrible, worthless, very bad person.

Sound ridiculous? Maybe it's a bit of an exaggeration, but we do it all the time. We don't know the reason someone acted the way they did, and we make up a motive that has no basis in reality. It might suit our mood, or our current level of insecurity, or maybe our flair for the dramatic.

How many times has your spouse or significant other seemed a bit distant and you've attributed it to anger, lack of interest, or smoldering resentment because you failed to wash your lunch dishes? When the truth is that he is just trying to remember the name of his eighth-grade math teacher—and it's driving him crazy that he can't.

Many, many years ago, I learned that the board of directors of an organization for which I served as executive director held a board meeting without telling me. I stewed for twenty-four hours. Why would they meet without me? Had I done something terrible they needed to talk about without me present? Were they going to fire me? Finally, I picked up the phone and called the board president. I explained that association boards should never meet without the knowledge and presence of their executive director. It was my job to make sure they never violated any antitrust regulations or nonprofit laws. What, I asked, could possibly have motivated them to hold a meeting without me? There was a long pause at the other end of the line. A very long pause.

Finally Doug said, "We do know that, Donna, and ordinarily we'd never meet without telling you, but our conference is coming up, and we wanted to honor you for the great job you are doing for us. We were talking about the best time to have a special ceremony and what we could buy you for a thank-you gift."

I felt like bug spit.

Ever since that embarrassing moment, I've tried to imagine positive reasons for inexplicable actions rather than negative ones. My positive stories are often just as erroneous as my negative ones, but while I'm in that suspended limbo of not knowing, why not enjoy my imaginings rather than agonize and fret over them?

Kindness Lessons

There are some great kindness lessons for us if we take time to think about how we feel and what we do when we have gaps in our knowledge.

Lesson #1: It's not always about us . . . in fact, it's usually *not* about us. Just because we're the center of our own universe, it's very unlikely we hold that exalted position in many other minds. I find this reminder immensely freeing: "Forget what everyone else thinks of you; chances are they aren't thinking about you at all."

Lesson #2: Yield to the curiosity triggered by not knowing. Employ curiosity to seek kind and compassionate answers to gaps in our knowledge. When we remain open and curious, there's no place for anger and resentment—but there is, remarkably, always a space for kindness.

Lesson #3: Assume one another's good intent. Instead of attributing a silence or an ill-chosen word to malice or resentment, we can just as easily say to ourselves, "That didn't come out the way she meant it to, but I know her intention was positive." Why wouldn't we want to believe the best rather than the worst?

Lesson #4: We always have a choice about the stories we make up. Even if we are drama queens and kings, we can make up stories based on positive assumptions. All it takes is some awareness on our part.

Lesson #5: We can always choose peace. We have control over both our perceptions and our reactions. We can choose the path that leads us to peace. It takes practice, but it's within our capabilities.

The stories we tell ourselves have power. With a little awareness, we can harness that power—and change our lives, perhaps even the world.

Kindness in Action: When was the last time you made up a story to fill a gap in your knowledge? Was it a positive story or a negative one? What are you going to do next time? Can you think of a time when you made an assumption about someone or something that was so off-base that you laugh (or cringe) just thinking about it? Do you sometimes feel immobilized by self-consciousness? Does it help to realize that you really aren't being judged—everyone else is too busy worrying about how they are being perceived? Next time you find yourself filling in a gap in knowledge with your imagination, use the opportunity to craft the most positive story you can imagine, or the one that brings you the most peace.

Chapter 34:

What Are You Looking For (Really)?

"When given the choice between being right or being kind, choose kind." (R. J. Palacio)

I tried to approach my year of living kindly as an opportunity for me to practice kindness and to learn to extend kindness more often and more naturally. It was also an opportunity for me to expand my kindness awareness, to see others acting kindly and recognize the act for what it is.

I expected to observe many incidents of unkindness or of missed opportunities for kindness—and that many would likely be my own—but I didn't want to spend my time looking for or focused on those negative examples. As José Ortega y Gasset said, "Tell me what you pay attention to, and I will tell you who you are."

This approach to life doesn't come naturally to me. The example my mother set was very different. As a result of her own life experiences growing up, she learned to distrust people; her default setting was that people were not to be relied upon and were to be kept at a distance until they proved themselves worthy of her trust. She approached new situations in much the same way, with the expectation that there was something lurking to harm her or—at the very least—to disappoint her. The messages I grew up with were: *Life isn't safe—proceed cautiously,* and *If given the chance, most people will take advantage of you, so don't let them get too close.*

Despite my mother's example, it has been my experience that the world is not out to get me. For the most part, in our day-to-day lives, we get what we expect. If I expect to be treated with courtesy and respect, I generally am, and I am greatly surprised to be treated otherwise. Of course, I am saying this as a middle-aged, middle-class, white woman. I am not so naive that I don't realize I could be treated very differently if I were of a different age, race, gender, background, or circumstance. Far too many people still react out of prejudice, fear, and ignorance. Nonetheless, choosing to be a person who expects the best—of herself and others—is a way to cultivate the world as we want it to be.

When What We Do Gets in the Way of Who We Are

There are a lot of people—smart, generous, and kind—whose professions have trained them to look for what's wrong and rewarded them for their efforts. In our company—managing nonprofit organizations—we saw this with certain clients over the years. If success in their profession requires that they be good at finding mistakes, aberrations, or imprecision—as building inspectors, clinical diagnosticians, or auditors, for example—they sometimes extend that ability to other parts of their lives, often completely unaware that it may not be appropriate or appreciated. They are always the ones to point out the typo in the newsletter. They find fault with the way the hedge was clipped or the lawn was mowed. They feel the need to inform their waitress in the Thai restaurant that "Wellcome" is misspelled on the menu. (Let's you and I move to Bangkok and open a restaurant and see if we get everything right!)

Sadly, they spend their lives listening for the missed note rather than for the music.

Sometimes, with only a few words, they can suck the life and joy out of an encounter. They're "just trying to help" by pointing out a flaw, but the person they've pointed it out to can be annoyed, demoralized, and even demotivated. We saw the damage such behaviors wreak in a boardroom; I can only imagine what having such a critical person as a spouse or parent might be like.

The lesson here may be that qualities that make someone good at their job may not be the same skills that make them a good parent, colleague, friend, or board member. Sometimes, the kindest thing we can do is overlook the unimportant blunder, the mispronunciation, the misstatement. It's hard, though, if you've been trained to seek out flaws, or if it's important to you that everyone knows how smart you are. I think it sometimes comes down to *would you rather be right or happy?* . . . because you can't always be both. This is one of those lessons we learn and relearn, and one of those choices we must make and then make again and again.

An editor friend of mine once told me he finds it hard at times to read for pleasure, because he can't turn off the editor in his head. He finds himself looking for errors or better ways to craft a sentence rather than enjoying the author's passion or the story.

Wayne Muller, in one of my favorite books, *How, Then, Shall We Live?*[1] (a source for many of the quotes that open these chapters) elegantly describes the dangers of honing our critical skills to the exclusion of others: "All we are is a result of what we have thought. If we focus the lion's share of our energy on ferreting out what we believe is wrong inside us, we gradually grow into people who are good at seeing what is wrong. . . . Instead of creating a life of beauty and meaning, we may simply become better and better at seeing only what is broken."

Focusing our lives on what's broken isn't a very satisfying way to live, nor is it likely to result in a good death, unless, of course, one wants their last words to be, "I told you so."

Choosing Peace

We can choose not only how we wish to see the world but also how we wish to interact with it. In her wonderful book *Grace (Eventually): Thoughts on Faith*[2], the irreverently devout Anne Lamott tells a story of having been swindled by a carpet salesman. She bought a rug for her church that turned out to be moldy and unusable. After days of increasingly rancorous back-and-forth to recover the fifty dollars she spent, Lamott decides to choose peace over victory. She returns the "carpet guy's" bad check with a note of apology and a bouquet of daisies. Even then, the carpet guy gets in one last jab—chiding her for behaving badly. Rather than point out just how badly *he* had acted, and the fact that she was still out fifty dollars with no rug to show for it, Anne lets it go.

Reading Lamott's story led me to wonder how I would behave in the same circumstance. Would I relinquish the notion that someone (me) has to be right and someone (the other guy) has to be wrong? Would I give up the satisfaction of having the last word? Would I surrender fifty dollars—or five dollars—that was rightfully mine to gain peace of mind and perspective? Would I trade righteousness for harmony?

I've been thinking a lot about how I have responded in the past and am likely to respond in the future when sharp words, criticism, or belittling comments are directed at me. I hope I will choose wisely from among the following:

- I can respond in kind ("tit for tat"); I can be equally sharp or critical: "That's the stupidest thing I've ever heard." There's a good chance this would escalate the situation.
- Or I can respond in such a way that indicates my superiority, showing that I'm above the other person's petty criticism: "What a shame that you have to resort to name-calling." Implied here is *I feel sorry for you, you under-evolved oaf.* That may not further escalate the situation, but the other person will still feel like I've dropped a warm turd in his hand.

- I can completely ignore the person and their words or actions. It may be a safe response—especially if the other person is psychotic or deranged—but it does little to improve things. Again, this message suggests my superiority: "I can't be bothered acknowledging your existence." *That's* not going to improve things!

- I can also acknowledge my fear and my pride and think about how I might connect with the other person where their fear and pride reside. I can say, "I'm sorry you feel that way, and I'm sorry if I did anything to annoy you. I'll try to be more aware next time." The thing is, I have to mean it. This can be where confrontation ends and reconciliation begins. However, if I say it with a tone that conveys sarcasm or superiority, or insincerity, we're right back in turd territory. It doesn't work if the whole time I'm saying it I'm resenting the fact that I have to admit I may be wrong when I *know* I am right. I have to be willing to stay silent and hold to my intent—even if their response is condescending, critical, or a clearly intended jab.

This takes practice and can be clumsy and awkward at first, sometimes resulting in all the things we hope to avoid. But, just like playing the piano or hitting a tennis ball, it takes some practice before we start seeing skill development. I comfort myself with wisdom from Julia Cameron: "It's impossible to get better and look good at the same time."

I don't recall instances in recent years when someone verbally attacked me and I attacked back. That's just not my style. I'm too "nice" for that. But there were times—sadly, too many—where I acted with indifference, disdain, and even superiority. Generally, my response was in answer to what I *perceived* from the other person—be they family, friend, colleague, service worker, or complete stranger. Perceptions aren't always accurate, and I have control over both my perceptions and my reactions. This, we've seen, is where kindness resides.

Surrender doesn't necessarily mean giving up or letting go. I think it can mean *opening up* or *letting something in*. That's what Anne Lamott did with her shady carpet guy. Viewed that way, I find it becomes easier to choose the kind response. I'm not capitulating; I'm not weak. I am allowing my better self to emerge, and giving voice and strength to my kindness. I am choosing peace.

Kindness in Action: *How do you typically approach a new experience or a new acquaintance? Do you expect it to go well, or do you anticipate impediments? Do you tend to look for something to criticize or find fault with, or do you make an effort to appreciate the best of the person or the experience? Are you able to initially trust people, reserving judgment until their behavior demonstrates otherwise? Over the next couple of days, simply pay attention to the attitude you carry into your interactions and your anticipation of them, and think about what might be their motivation—fear, insecurity, the need to be right . . . Then, if you notice that you're focused on the negative, aim to change your expectations.*

Can you think of a time when you chose to be right rather than to be happy or at peace? Try to reenvision the situation with a different response and a different outcome. Can you see where choosing kindness—even if you lose an argument or a few dollars—is really an act of strength and courage? See what it feels like next time you are in a disagreement with your friend, coworker, family member, or a stranger, if you graciously concede and let them have the point. Did it feel like you lost something, or gained something?

III. Dealing with Unkindness

Chapter 35:

Big Bullies

"Look into your own heart, discover what it is that gives you pain, and then refuse, under any circumstance whatsoever, to inflict that pain on anybody else." (Karen Armstrong)

Even the best of us can have a bad day and act or speak unkindly. I'll bet even Mother Teresa had a snarky moment or two. But consistent, repeated, and unrepentant unkindness is more than a slip or a slide. It's often the sign of a bully.

In general, people who are chronically unkind behave as they do out of a misplaced sense of entitlement, or uncontrolled anger, or—as often as not—fear. They may feel threatened, or they may be afraid of rejection or embarrassment, or of appearing weak or stupid.

Many years ago I worked with an angry man who boasted quite openly that his philosophy of life was what he called "I.O." It stood for "instant offense." In any interaction, this fellow wanted to have the upper hand, so he immediately sought ways to put the person he was interacting with on the defensive.

He was a large man, a former ballplayer, and he knew his size could intimidate. But if that wasn't enough, he'd ask questions to put someone on the spot, or he'd dismiss their words with a derisive comment and a roll of his eyes. He knew how to look a person up and down and convey to them that he found them lacking. I didn't realize it at the time, but he was simply a bully.

All these years later, I find myself wondering what he was afraid of. Did he fear that someone would see through his facade and recognize the insecure man inside? Had he not lived up to expectations—his own or someone else's—and decided to cover up his disappointment by attacking others before they could recognize the truth about him? Perhaps he had been hurt deeply and decided he could avoid a repeat of that experience by inflicting hurt first. Maybe he had been taught that this is how "real men" behave. Or maybe he was simply an unrepentant jerk who enjoyed tormenting and intimidating others.

I avoided him whenever possible and fortunately didn't have all that many occasions to interact with him in the company we worked for. It would be interesting to encounter him today and see if the passage of time has mellowed him.

According to the website www.bullyingstatistics.org,[1] "Adult bullies were often either bullies as children or bullied as children." The site further describes five types of adult bullies:

1. **Narcissistic Adult Bully:** This type of adult bully is self-centered and does not share empathy with others. Additionally, they feel little anxiety about consequences. They seem to feel good about themselves but in reality have a brittle narcissism that requires putting others down.

2. **Impulsive Adult Bully:** Adult bullies in this category are more spontaneous and don't really plan out their bullying. Even if consequences are likely, this bully has a hard time restraining his or her behavior. In some cases, this type of bullying may be unintentional, resulting from periods of stress.

3. Physical Bully: While adult bullying rarely turns to physical confrontation, there are, none-theless, bullies who use physicality. In some cases, the adult bully may not actually physically harm the victim, but may use a looming threat of harm or physical domination. Physical bullying might also mean taking or destroying someone's property rather than a physical confrontation.

4. Verbal Adult Bully: Words can be quite dam-aging. Adult bullies who use this type of tactic may start rumors about the victim, or use sarcastic or demeaning language to dominate or humiliate another person.

5. Secondary Adult Bully: This is someone who does not initiate the bullying but joins in so that he or she does not become another victim down the road. Secondary bullies may feel bad about what they are doing, but they are more concerned about protecting themselves.

The website contends that there is little one can do about an adult bully, "because adult bullies are often in a set pattern. They are not interested in working things out, and they are not interested in compromise. Rather, adult bullies are more interested in power and domination. They want to feel as though they are important and preferred, and they accomplish this by bringing others down."

I'm not willing to concede that easily. I think there must be ways to stand up to bullies and let them know their behavior is not acceptable, and to do so without resorting to their own tactics of threatening or berating—which only show them the power of bullying. Trying to shame a bully by embarrassing or berating them will probably have the effect of increasing their bullying tendencies. Like my office colleague from so many years ago, they will go into "instant offense" mode and strike wherever they see a likely target.

I don't think kindness would have been an effective deterrent to that colleague's bullying. He would probably have equated kindness with weakness and flexed his muscles all the more.

What might have been effective would have been for witnesses to let him know his behavior was unacceptable. Instead of remaining silent, colleagues and peers should have stepped in and calmly said, "Not cool, buddy." Most bullies will back down—or at least back off—if they see witnesses rallying to support their victim.

Perhaps the smartest thing to do when one is the target of a bully is to get out. Don't engage; don't react in kind. Simply exit and avoid future interactions. But, of course, that's not always possible. Sometimes the bullies in our lives are people we cannot avoid. We must never allow bullying to become abuse—whether we are the direct target of the perpetrator or a witness. There's no shame in asking for help if you are faced with a bully or an abuser.

I keep thinking about the old adage that the best revenge is a good life, and that's probably a good way to look at bullying in the long term. But when one is actively being bullied or harassed, it does little good to think, "Hey, sport, in ten years I'll have a great life, and you'll still be a colossal jerk."

If we are not the bully's target but find ourselves in the position of witness or bystander, we need to step in and let the perpetrator know—in no uncertain terms—that such behavior is unacceptable. Psychopaths and maniacs are to be seriously avoided, but your garden-variety bully might be tempered with judicious words and assertive confidence. If we can step in without expressing anger or contempt, we may be able to defuse the situation.

Kindness requires action, and it often requires courage. When we witness bullying, we can't ignore it and just be a bystander. Bullying is fostered by silence. We need to step in, speak up, and stand for what we know to be right. That's easier said than done, but kindness isn't always easy. *It is, though, always right.* Collectively, we all must condemn bullying. It's not normal, it's not manly, it's not acceptable. Period.

Kindness in Action: *Have you encountered any bullies in your adult life—in your workplace, your neighborhood, or even your family? Whether you or someone else is their target, can you see any way to defuse their behavior? Can you acknowledge the strength of your own kindness even if another person chooses to demean it? Recognizing that safety is paramount, think about possible ways to respond next time you see or experience bullying. Strategize how you would stand up for yourself or for someone who is being harassed by a bully. Talk about this with children or others in your life who may face similar choices.*

Chapter 36:

Little Bullies: Where It All Begins

It's one thing to be an adult dealing with bullies—we have more options, more experience, more perspective, and more power—but children facing bullying can be devastated by it, and face lifelong consequences as a result.

As I explore kindness, it's been alarming to see how frequently bullying comes up—adult bullying as well as bullying by and of children and adolescents. It's frightening so see the long-term destructive effects of those behaviors. The vast majority of adult bullies were also bullies as children, or else they themselves were bullied or abused. The earlier we address and counter bullying, the better the chances of preventing it or breaking its cycle.

Jenny Hulme, author of *How to Create Kind Schools*[1], notes that bullying is not and should not be considered "just part of growing up." As she explains, "Bullying brings no benefits at all—either to the bully or the bullied. It can, instead, trigger a cycle of victimization that can last a lifetime. Studies have shown victims of bullying, including very able children, stand a much lower chance of doing well at school and are more likely to experience depression, anxiety, and poor physical health as adults."[2]

I don't remember there being a lot of bullying in my childhood—of course, one of the benefits of aging is selective memory. Throughout my elementary school years, there were two boys whom I recall being tormenters; they picked on smaller boys and strutted around like bantamweight princes. I don't think we called them bullies, though perhaps the boys they picked on did. Neither boy was very bright; I supposed their bad behavior may have been their way of dealing with the fact that intelligence was rewarded at our elementary school, and they struggled to keep up with their fellow fourth graders.

Bullying today is scary. It's practiced and experienced by both boys and girls. It goes beyond taunts on the playground—which are bad enough—to organized hazing through social media and unimaginable cruelty. Cyberbullying, especially, isn't something that occurs and is then forgotten. It flourishes on social media sites, it gets forwarded, it takes on a life of its own.

Bullying takes many forms. What starts out as playground taunting might escalate later into sexual harassment, gang activity, domestic violence, workplace intimidation, or elder abuse. The sooner we make it clear to all that *any* form of bullying is unacceptable, and the sooner we help bullies learn other behaviors, the sooner we will see declines in these offenses.

Stories are everywhere of the devastating effects of bullying. Jacki James recounts the long-term bullying her son Peyton was subjected to, which eventually led to his suicide. We hear other stories of the quiet kids who were bullied for years before they snapped and turned a rifle on their persecutors, bystanders, and then themselves.

After her son's suicide, Jacki James became an activist for kindness and to counter bullying. She created the website www. kindness-matters.org, which seeks to change the ways people interact with one another and to foster kindness on a global level. Ms. James explains that "Children bully others because it gives them a sense of power that they are otherwise missing in their lives. Many times, a bully will be the victim in a different situation, maybe at home or on a team. So to make up for their lack of self-worth, they lash out at others to give themselves power in that situation. It is a way of deflecting how they really feel about themselves onto someone else."[3]

Bullies, according to Ms. James, need to understand the damage their words can inflict. "They need to understand that they don't know the demons another person is fighting, and just because the person they've abused smiles or laughs, that doesn't mean they're okay. It just means they're hiding their true feelings and either holding it all inside or lashing out at another time." She cautions that no one wants to carry the guilt of saying something cruel and later learning that they were the last person to speak to another who took his or her own life. "That is a guilt that will tear you up, little by little, every day for the rest of your life."

Thirty percent of middle- and high-school students report having been bullied, and more than half the girls in grades seven through twelve report experiencing sexual harassment in school. These are more than statistics—they represent millions of children and young people who face each day with fear and despair of ever feeling safe. There are those who say bullying is a childhood "rite of passage." That's just wrong—as wrong as wrong can be—and it's up to us as adults to do everything we can to protect children—all children.

It seems pretty obvious that kindness is something we learn—or don't learn—as children. And then what we learn—or don't—accompanies us into adulthood, where we become kind adults, bullies, or sometimes bystanders.

It is up to us . . . are we up to it?

Kindness in Action: *Were you bullied as a child, or perhaps sometimes a bully? Did you see other children bullied? What were the messages from your childhood, and have they stayed with you? If you have children, have you talked to them about bullying? More important, have you listened to them? Open a dialogue with your child about kindness, about playground behaviors and cyber-behaviors, as well as all the strong and powerful reasons to choose kindness. What are they learning in school, and how can you help them understand the respect that is due every individual? Many schools have put kindness and anti-bullying programs in their curriculum. Check to see whether your child's school has these programs—and maybe even if they need some adult volunteers.*

Chapter 37:

Bystanding ... or Standing Up

for Kindness?

"It is only with true love and compassion that we can begin to mend what is broken in the world. It is these two blessed things that can begin to heal all broken hearts." (Steve Maraboli)

We hear and read an alarming number of stories of bigotry and intimidation all over the world—in playgrounds, on college campuses, and in towns and cities of all sizes. People are angry. People are frightened. There are those who believe they are superior or entitled, and those who make themselves feel big by belittling others—usually people who are smaller or weaker, or different. Experts have plenty of theories explaining such behavior—fear, ignorance, inferiority complex, blind devotion to a charismatic despot, and more. While it's important to recognize and understand why such people think and act as they do, our purpose here is to think about how we will react when we encounter such behaviors.

Standing by silently can give tacit approval to a bully or tormentor. Stepping in to defend someone who is being harassed might put us at risk, too—of physical or verbal abuse. What's the right thing to do? And how do we do it right?

Maybe you won't ever be witness to an actual hate crime, but you are likely to encounter hateful speech and bigoted actions. How you respond can change the dynamic. Psychology tells us that people tend to get their cues for how to behave from the others around them. If one person immediately confronts a bully—not in a hostile way, but firmly and self-assuredly—others will follow suit. Often it just takes one person willing to be the first to stand up.

It's wise to think about these situations before they happen. Picture yourself speaking out. How would you stand? What would you say? What does it feel like to stand up for what you believe? I haven't found myself in an extremely confrontational situation yet, but there have been circumstances where I've been in conversation with people who express intolerant opinions or display a prejudice. At one time, I may have remained silent, my jaw tightening in disapproval, silently vowing never to interact with this individual again. And I'd look around me and see others wearing the same expression of disgust or disdain. Now, though, I will speak out. I try to do it respectfully and without belittling the offender. Often, I will employ curiosity: "What makes you think that?" "Where did you get that information?" Or I will try to appeal to reason: "Here's another way to look at that . . ." "Is it fair to judge an entire group by the behavior of one person?" "Here's where my experience differs from yours . . ."

Stepping in to express curiosity might also work if we find ourselves a spectator when another person is being bullied or tormented. Reason may not influence the bully, but it may move other bystanders to step forward. Take some time to think about how you might respond. Practice saying the words out loud. Have this conversation with your family—especially children—and encourage them to be prepared with a strategy to stand up to bullies.

Psychologist Philip Zimbardo, author of *The Lucifer Effect*[1], says, "For anyone to become an active, everyday social hero who does daily deeds of helping and compassion, that journey and new role in life begins in one's mind."[2]

It's a great place to start.

The vast majority of young people are not bullies and are not bullied. They're bystanders, and this, I suspect, is where efforts need to be focused to make bullying a thing of the past.

It's true with adults, too. We see bullying in the workplace, or perhaps on the sports field or the mall parking lot, and we don't like it, but we don't know how to intervene.

In the discussion of bullying—whether children, adolescents, or adults—the key to countering the abuse is motivating bystanders to step in and act in support of the person being bullied.

According to Megan Kelley Hall, coeditor of *Dear Bully: Seventy Authors Tell Their Stories*[3], "The bystander definitely has the power to help change the climate—with adults and children. In bullying cases with children, almost half of all bullying situations stop when a bystander gets involved."[4] She further explains that getting involved "doesn't mean taking a stand or getting into the bully's face, sometimes just the simple act of not giving the bully an audience or just taking the side of the victim is enough to get your point across."

Helpful and Hurtful Bystanders

The website www.eyesonbullying.org[5] describes both hurtful and helpful bystanders. The former instigate or encourage the bully, or sometimes they join in once bullying has begun. Sometimes they may not actively support the bullying behavior, but through their passive acceptance they condone the torment and offer the bully the audience he or she craves.

Helpful bystanders assess the situation and then directly intervene by defending the victim or redirecting the situation; alternatively, they may get help from others present to stand up to or discourage the bully, or report the bullying to someone in authority who can intervene.

Why We Don't Step Forward

The site also describes some of the reasons why bystanders don't intervene. Among them:

- They fear being hurt or becoming the target of the bully themselves.
- They feel powerless to stop the bully.
- They think it's none of their business.
- They don't want to draw attention to themselves.
- They fear retribution.
- They fear that telling adults won't help and may make the situation worse.
- They don't know what to do.

What to Do

The bystander's reaction will set the tone for other witnesses and may serve to enlighten the bully without embarrassing or shaming them. Perhaps it will give them a means of exiting the encounter without feeling put down. Maybe—just maybe—it will teach them that there are more effective ways to behave—ways they haven't learned at home and aren't likely to. Silence and inaction sustain bullying. Whether the setting is the schoolyard, the workplace, social or recreational situations, or cyberspace, bullying must be stopped. The vast majority of us, who are neither bullied nor bullies, have the responsibility to step in when we see bullying or other forms of cruelty. We need to say, "No more!" and model the world as we would like it to be.

It's good to remember that everyone—bully, victim, and bystander—carries an invisible and heavy load. Perhaps one of the best reasons we are all here on this planet is to help others shoulder the weight of their load—even if we can't see it and don't know what it is.

The website www.bullying.org[6] offered some excellent advice on what kids should do if they see someone else being bullied. Much of that advice is directly related to kindness. It suggests befriending a child who is being bullied—talk to them, walk with them, eat lunch with them. Make an effort to involve or extend an invitation to the new kid in school or the kids who often seem to be alone. Don't try to respond in kind to a bully—don't fight them, make fun of them, or say mean things back at them—it usually makes things worse.

This is where parents and schools, and even the media, can help. If we have discussions about what to do when we witness bullying, we'll be better prepared to act, rather than be paralyzed by fear, confusion, or uncertainty. If kids—or adults—know that they can make a difference and are aware of strategies for intervening, they will be much more likely to do so.

Education Is Key

Research into bystanding indicates that people who are educated about compassion or provided strategies for helping others are more likely to step in to help someone who is being bullied. Kids need to learn that bullying isn't cool, and it isn't acceptable. They need to learn it at home, at school, from the media, and from their peers. And kids who are the target of bullies need to understand that there's nothing wrong with them, and there's nothing wrong with being different—it's the bully who has the problem and the bully who needs fixing.

Schools and parents need to take seriously their responsibility to teach kids that it's not enough not to be a bully, we must all be willing to step in when we see bullying and let the perpetrator know it's not acceptable. That takes courage, and courage—like kindness—is a capacity that strengthens with practice.

Instead of standing by, let's all stand up for what's right.

Kindness in Action: If you're a parent, have a talk with your child about bullying and help him or her strategize how they will respond the next time they witness bullying. And do the same for yourself—whether you encounter it in the workplace, on the bus, or at a community meeting. Think about what you might say and how you will stand and speak with confidence. Knowing in advance how we want to behave helps us to follow through when the circumstance arises.

Chapter 38:

Choosing Our Cyber-Voices and

Media Companions

"The true essence of humankind is kindness. There are other qualities which come from education or knowledge, but it is essential, if one wishes to be a genuine human being and impart satisfying meaning to one's existence, to have a good heart." (Dalai Lama)

I grew up in a time when name-calling was something that occurred on a playground and was generally quickly forgotten. Things said in the heat of the moment were overlooked, as they should be. I'm not saying that my childhood was an idyllic world where there was no bullying or cruelty. But we had nothing to compare with the devastating force of today's online bullying. Cyberbullying has taken bullying to new and insidious heights. I've been stunned and dismayed to learn about the extent of it and the number of suicides and attempted suicides it has triggered—mostly in children and teens. This ultimate unkindness must be stopped.

In an excellent article from the November/December 2014 issue of *Scientific American Mind* entitled "Virtual Assault,"[1] author Elizabeth Svoboda described the many ways people are bullied online or through social media, and the psychology of people who engage in such poisonous activities. She noted, interestingly, that "contrary to popular wisdom, bullies are not merely compensating for their own low self-esteem," but often they are "perched at the *top* of the social hierarchy and demean others to cement their position."

People who engage in cyberbullying and attacking others online or through social media are often referred to as "trolls." It's up to the online community, says Svoboda, to establish norms and tell trolls in no uncertain terms that bullying is not acceptable. She also says one way to counter the damage of bullying is to step in and offer support to the victim. Silence isn't golden.

It isn't just speaking up or weighing in. Another aspect of supporting kindness electronically is being mindful about what we click.

We can change the unkindness being spread online and through social media by not clicking on it. Not clicking when we see a venomous, cruel, or provocative headline; not clicking when we encounter gossip or negative articles and message boards. It's that simple: we manifest what we give our attention to, and if our attention is on the cruel and the crude, it will foster more of the same. There are individuals and internet sites that are deliberately vicious. They engage in deliberate lies, name-calling, body-shaming, intimidation, and racist, sexist, or other narrow-minded bigotry. They thrive because people give them attention. People click on them, they follow links, they comment. Even when the comments are to disagree with the haters, it gives them power: they can hate more and respond more aggressively. It's a perversity I don't understand and probably never will. I've started to think of my clicks as fuel: if I click on sites that foster hate or spread hurtful or silly gossip, these things will proliferate and bring more negativity to a world already swamped with negativity. But if I don't click, and you don't, and thousands or millions of others say, "Enough!" and stop clicking, they will eventually fade away to their rightful obscurity. I have to believe that.

Likewise, we can foster a positive and healthy cyberspace by choosing kindness, making kind comments, and taking the time to encourage rather than berate. With every click, we make a choice. What an important choice it is!

When I started planning and setting up my blog—a complete novice of the form—I read a couple of books and a number of articles about blogging. I also talked to a few experienced bloggers. Out of the many pieces of excellent advice I got, there was one I chose to ignore.

Everyone said to set up the blog so I could moderate comments before they went public, or at least moderate the first comment someone makes; then, if I approved their comment, that individual was "preapproved" for future comments. The other option was viewed as dangerous: to allow any comments to appear without an opportunity to weed out the crackpots and the haters.

WordPress is a great platform, and it gives the novice blogger plenty of guidance and plenty of options. During setup, I clicked the button that allows comments to appear without any moderation. It seemed to me if I were going to commit to kindness, I needed to trust that any readers who might visit the blog and take the time to comment would have good intent. I haven't regretted it. I will also admit, though, that I did think that if anyone posted a rude or malicious message, it would give me an opportunity to test my kindness resolve—could I be gracious and compassionate if attacked online?

Without exception, the comments readers have made have been thoughtful, wise, and also kind. They've inspired me to think, sometimes to laugh, and *always* to feel grateful for the time commenters have taken to share their thoughts. If there are crackpots out there, I haven't encountered them.

There is much positivity to be found on the internet. It enriches our lives in so many ways. That's why I'm still so surprised when I hear about the cruelty and malice some people engage in—usually anonymously. I don't understand it; perhaps I never will. But if enough of us click mindfully and choose kindness, perhaps the unkind voices will someday be stilled.

Somewhat related, think about whether the movies you see and the shows you watch on television are contributing to a kind world. My husband and I realized a few years ago that we were watching some shows that didn't leave us feeling good or happy. They were often highly rated programs, with great actors and compelling stories. But frequently there wasn't one character in a show we could like. If not downright evil, characters were unpleasant and conniving. They were not people we would want as friends, and, in fact, might be people we would go out of our way to avoid having to interact with. So why were we inviting them into our home every week? We decided we didn't want their energy in our house. And it raised the question: Does watching meanness make us more inclined to be mean or accepting of unkind behavior?

Admittedly, there are some very good programs we've chosen not to watch because of the violence, negativity, or obnoxious nature of the characters. We're probably missing some quality television. It's not something I would tell others to do—these are personal decisions—but I do suggest that whatever we choose to watch we do so mindfully, aware of why we are watching, what messages are being sent, and what we can learn.

__Kindness in Action:__ Next time you're tempted to click on some salacious celebrity gossip or on a link that promises the lowdown on a public figure, pause to think about whether you really want to support the spreading of such information (or, more likely, misinformation). If people stop clicking, negative sites may start to go away. If you see someone being trolled on the web, speak out and say, "That's not okay." Or if that feels too risky, send the victim a private message of support and encouragement. When you read positive content online, take a moment to send a message to the author or provide a kind comment. And when you read something that angers

you, think about what response is best for you and best for the world. Ask yourself what your cyber-voice is and what you want it to be.

If there are kids in your life, talk with them about cyber-behavior. Make sure they understand that comments made online can be just as cruel and hurtful as face-to-face bullying—maybe even more so. What may seem harmless or funny could have catastrophic results. Lastly, have a conversation with your family about the TV shows you're watching and the energy and messages they're sending. You don't need to restrict what you watch—unless you want to—but be aware of what and whom you are inviting into your home.

Chapter 39:

Dancing with Yes: Dance Like

No One's Watching

"If you have to choose between being kind and being right, choose being kind and you will always be right." *(Anonymous)*

et's check in again about how kindness is manifesting in your life. Are you more aware of the various forms of kindness all around you—big and small, dramatic and subtle? Do you recognize unkindness more readily, and are you more able to respond to it in positive ways? None of us are going to become perfect givers or receivers of kindness—saints are few and far between—but as long as you're progressing in the direction of kindness and away from indifference and unkindness, you are strengthening the kindness community. You may not be noticing all the changes in your life or even in your thinking or behavior, but you can be sure that they're happening.

There are still likely to be areas that especially challenge you or push your buttons—perhaps a certain person in whose presence your teeth grind, or a particular circumstance that always seems to ignite a short, inner fuse. Recognizing these triggers is a big step toward neutralizing them. If kindness is growing in your awareness, does it feel good and right to you? Has anyone commented on your actions or words—acknowledging that you've made a positive difference? Even if no one else has noticed, take a moment to commend yourself for contributing to a kinder world, and to imagine all the ways your kindness is rippling outward (to three degrees of separation, as we saw in Chapter 5)—to people you have never met and places you have never been. Don't ever let anyone tell you kindness is weak or it doesn't make a difference. You know better; you've seen its power.

Reflecting back on recent chapters, consider these questions and key points:

- Has it taken courage to extend a kindness—perhaps because you felt awkward, or uncertain how the other person would respond, or because it made you feel embarrassed or vulnerable? Each time you overcome misgivings and hesitation to extend kindness, you claim your own innate courage—and nobody can take it from you!
- Do you spend more time looking for what's right or for things to criticize? What do you pay the most attention to?
- Has going outside your comfort zone to extend kindness made you feel vulnerable? It can be a scary feeling, but can you overcome it, along with your quest for perfection, in order to be authentically kind and allow yourself to be fully seen?
- Is it more important to you to be right or happy? Can you sometimes master the difficult task of staying graciously silent when a disagreement escalates or cycles endlessly? If you have been able to, can you view your action as both a strength and a kindness? Good for you!

- When you lack information, do you tend to fill in the gaps with positive assumptions or conjectures that have a negative spin? Which give you more peace of mind? Are you making an effort to be actively curious when you encounter unkindness or the unknown?
- What are your "eulogy virtues"? What traits would you most like to be known and remembered by?
- Have you thought about how you will respond if you are ever a witness—or target—of bullying? If you have kids, have you had this conversation with them?
- What are you clicking on? As you surf the web or participate in social media, are you more aware that how you engage contributes to making the world a kinder, or an unkinder place?
- Remember that kindness is a choice we always have, and in making that choice, we exert our strength and support the world as we want it to be.

What else can you do to incorporate kindness into your life? No matter what may be going on in the world right now, take some time to appreciate the kindness all around you and especially your own contributions to creating a kinder world. What one new gesture or expression of kindness will you do today?

PART FOUR:

The Season
of Becoming

I. Challenges to Kindness

Chapter 40:

When My Kindness Is Your "Yuck!"

"Out beyond ideas of wrongdoing and rightdoing there is a field. I'll meet you there." (Rumi)

When my husband is sick, he wants to be left alone. He's like an animal that crawls off to die in seclusion. I would like to fuss over him, fluff his pillows, mop his brow, croon "poor baby," but that's not what he wants.

When I'm sick, I like a little attention—not a lot, just check in on me occasionally, make sure I'm still breathing, and see if I want some ginger ale or another blanket. Over the years, Bill has perfected exactly the right amount of solicitous attention to help me feel cared for but not smothered. A few degrees in either direction, and I would feel either neglected or pestered.

That's one of the challenges of kindness: learning to meet the other person's needs and not impose our own.

It's for this reason I've never been entirely comfortable with the "golden rule," which says, "Do unto others as you would have them do unto you"—a sentiment promulgated by nearly every major religion. The problem is that what I may want in certain circumstances may not be what another person wants. If I always go by what I'd like, it's quite probable I won't meet the other person's needs.

For example, I tend to be a fairly private, low-key person. As a rule, I don't like to be the center of attention (the exception being when I have a microphone in my hand). I'm not comfortable with effusive thanks or extravagant praise. But I know other people who are—who welcome it and thrive on it. Were I to follow the golden rule, I would treat them with the reserve that I prefer for myself. My preferences aren't everyone's preferences, though, and if lavish and unrestrained praise are what my friend craves, that really is what I want to offer him.

The "platinum rule" says, "Treat others the way they want to be treated." That requires more mindfulness on our part, and an ability to be empathetic. We also risk guessing wrongly. "I thought for sure she'd like being serenaded by the high-school marching band for her birthday, but it turned out she would have preferred a quiet dinner for two." Oops!

Another example: I don't like surprises. They leave me tongue-tied and inspire a sort of "fight or flight" response. If something wonderful is coming my way, I want to know about it well in advance so I can savor not only the experience but also the anticipation of it. And, if it's something not so wonderful coming my way, I want to know about that, too, so I can be prepared and have time to think about how I will handle it. *I just don't like surprises.*

But I have friends who love surprises, and I would never deprive them of that pleasure simply because I don't understand or share the attraction. Under the platinum rule, I consider their desires and then help plan the surprise party. I may not agree, but I respect their preference and honor it, and hope they will do the same for me.

This is probably easier to do with people we know well. After a few years (maybe even decades) of trial and error, we understand their needs and wishes, and we know how to please.

It's harder with casual friends, colleagues, and acquaintances. We may make the mistake of assuming that what they'd like is the same as what we'd like.

It's even harder with strangers. How on earth can we know

what they want? I read a comment recently from a man who said he had ceased offering his seat on the bus to women, the elderly, or people who appeared to have a disability. After eight people refused his offer, displaying varying levels of offense that he thought they were incapable of standing, he resolved to keep his nose in his book and not offer again.

There's no question that it's awkward and uncomfortable when our attempts at kindness are rejected. I can also understand the point of view of the people who refused his kind offer—it may have made them feel weak or challenged their independence. As I think about how I might react in that situation, I'm guessing I might refuse, too (though graciously, I hope), thinking I don't need any special treatment and am perfectly capable of standing. The question becomes: Is it kinder to accept his offer or to allow him to keep his seat? It all depends on your perspective. No wonder people abandon civilization and make their homes in hermit caves. It's a whole lot easier than navigating social niceties in a complex world.

I wonder if there is a way to offer that makes it easier on everyone. Perhaps he could rise and say, "I would love to offer you my seat if you would consider taking it," accompanied by his most Cary Grant–like dazzling smile. (Who could refuse that?)

Knowing that our kindness may sometimes be unwelcome shouldn't deter us from extending kindness to the best of our ability and our judgment. It means never assuming we know what someone else wants, but asking. And, as we talked about in Chapter 19, if we are on the receiving end of misdirected or clumsy kindness, we need to be able to appreciate the intent, even if it missed the mark.

Kindness in Action: *Can you think of a time when a friend or relative assumed you would love something—because they did—and it left you cold? Have you ever been the giver in such a circumstance? Next time you think you know just the right choice for someone else, pause to think about whether you might be imposing your own preferences on them. When in doubt, ask!*

Chapter 41:

What If I Don't Feel Like Being Kind?

"You may be sorry that you spoke, sorry you stayed or went, sorry you won or lost, sorry so much was spent. But as you go through life, you'll find you're never sorry you were kind."
(Herbert Prochnow)

The more aware I am of my intention to be kind, the easier it is to choose kindness—even on those days when I just don't feel like it, or when it's hard, seems insignificant, or throws me off schedule. I frequently get calls from people who want to know more about careers in the nonprofit arena, or who are attracted by different facets of my profession: meeting planning, advocacy, public relations, communications, or working with volunteer leaders. Such calls often come when I'm on a tight deadline or already juggling a dozen tasks. Nonetheless, remembering how many people helped and mentored me as I advanced professionally, I nearly always try to make time for a meeting, coffee, or a long phone call. And I look for ways to help—an article or book that might further enlighten, an organization worth exploring, an introduction that might prove beneficial. In recent years, I've also tried to be proactive in offering help, realizing that some people may be too shy or reticent to ask for it. As I encounter young people entering my profession, I try to let them know that they are welcome to contact me for information or help.

Kindness isn't always tidy and straightforward. And it certainly isn't always easy. Sometimes it's inconvenient. Or it's awkward, bumbling, or misunderstood. Sometimes all we can do is guess, and hope that our kindness will have the result we intended. We can put it out there—how it is received is out of our control.

True kindness might also sometimes be *false* kindness in the sense that to be truly kind means extending kindness even when we may not feel it, and, in fact, when what we really want to do is say the snarkiest thing imaginable. Or when we just want to let the moment pass and pretend we didn't see the opportunity to be kind. This is when choosing kindness really means something.

Just as it's easy to be happy when the sun is shining and everything's going our way, it's easy to be kind when our kindness takes little effort, or when we know it will be appreciated, or when the recipient of our kindness is someone we know and like.

The key to true kindness—like the key to true happiness—is managing to maintain our attitude or keep our resolve when all hell is breaking loose. When the cat throws up all over a favorite sweater, the car is making a strange and worrisome noise, you've been on and off hold with customer support for over an hour, and a neighbor yells at you because all the leaves from your big tree blew into his yard.

When it's simply a crappy day, is just holding it together the best we can do, or can we move beyond our instant, emotional, and sometime automatic response and consciously choose the hard response, the one that we want to define us—the kind response?

Michael Broome put it well: "Character is when we have the discipline to follow through with the goal after the mood in which the goal was set passes."

I had a realization about halfway through my year of living kindly that my most important job—even more important than the job that generates my paycheck—is to be kind. When I took some time to slow down and think about what I was doing and how my life was changing, my heart felt full. It just felt so good to be kind; it felt so right to recognize the kindness that was all around me. It felt like I was making a difference, however small it may be. And that it is why I'm here, on the planet.

With that awareness, I see that the biggest kindness challenge is to be kind when I may not feel like it.

Learning to Pause Is Essential to Kindness

I recently read that "we drop into our reptilian brains when we feel threatened or angry"[1], which is where our survival responses are. These include attack, aggression, revenge, fear, and territorial behavior, among other instincts. Once in that primitive, reptilian state, it can take approximately twenty minutes to adjust back to our thinking and coping frontal lobes. And being kind from that reptilian state may not be possible. My friend Ann Macfarlane describes this state as "amygdala hijack"[2], when our brains respond to perceived threat with anger and rage.

We do have the ability to choose whether our higher brain is hijacked or taken over by reptilian instincts. We don't have to react instinctively or act on the first snarky impulse. If we can just learn to pause, we can choose who we are going to be in the next moment, and then the one after that. And we can always choose kindness. For me, I find it helps to visualize a reptile—an iguana or a crocodile—trying to climb into the driver's seat of my mind. I see myself opening the car door and pushing him out, gently but firmly, then driving on with a smile of satisfaction. Destination: kindness.

Also Essential: Maintaining Awareness

If we pay attention, we can probably avoid amygdala hijack. And then we can choose kindness, and the wonderful thing is that the experience of our own kindness will usually lift us out of our fury.

Another element of awareness is understanding why we want to be kind and how we want to respond to unkindness. Am I being kind to this person who was appallingly rude to me because I want to show them that I am better and more highly evolved? That they are wrong? That I will not stoop to their level? Or am I being kind to this person because I want to be kind no matter what, and because my kindness serves life— which is perfect in all its imperfections? More and more, when kindness is hard and I choose it anyway, it's for the latter reason. And the amazing thing is that it becomes easier and easier to choose kindness. I see that I'm not doing it for the other person or even despite the other person, I'm doing it for me—for who I want to be and what I want my life to look like. Life is something to be cherished, and no matter where I am, or however small I am, I can serve it.

Is Gossip Ever Kind?

Another form of unkindness that we can avoid by paying attention is indulging in the practice of gossip. It can be tempting to dish the dirt—we've all done it: talked about the absent colleague, the weird neighbor, the flaky relative. But it never feels good later; in fact, it feels icky. Instead, the kind response is to interrupt the spiraling cycle of gossip by saying, "Let's not talk about Genevieve behind her back," or "She handled that unhappy customer so well last week—I was really impressed by her professionalism, weren't you?" Or, at the very least, we can say, "I'm not comfortable with this conversation," and leave the room.

Sometimes we find ourselves in the middle of these sorts of conversations without realizing how we got here. That's where paying attention comes in. As soon as we start to get that uncomfortable feeling—for some of us it's in our stomachs, for others in our shoulders or neck, or a tightening in our throat—we need to think about what's not right here: Is this a conversation that diminishes rather than builds? Am I overlooking an opportunity to be kind? Am I burying my real feelings to be part of the group?

With regard to gossip, Peggy Drexler, PhD, writing for *Psychology Today*[3], explains, "Anthropologists believe that throughout human history, gossip has been a way for us to bond with others—and sometimes a tool to isolate those who aren't supporting the group."

Further, she notes that it's human nature for us to want to know about other people's lives—especially if we can somehow compare ourselves favorably to them: *She may have more money, but my marriage is happier.* Recognizing this might make it easier for us to acknowledge gossip when we see it or engage in it, and it also might help us to flip the tone, to change from catty to kind. We're aiming for improvement, not perfection.

It's not hard to be kind when I'm interacting with people I like, or when I'm energized and feeling good. But when I'm dealing with someone whom I find hard to like, or when I'm responding to rude behavior, or when I'm depleted or glum, kindness doesn't always burst forth like water from a hose. At best, it's a trickle. Extending kindness under these circumstances means taking the time to unkink the hose and allow kindness to flow unimpeded. Learning how to be kind when kindness isn't easy is one of the best lessons life offers us. It's one we learn over and over. And we do get better with practice.

On this never-ending path, the true challenge is to appreciate the moments when kindness might be hard, or when the object of our kindness pushes every one of our buttons—for these are the times when we can fully own our commitment to kindness, when we can say, "Choosing kindness wasn't easy . . . but I chose it anyway."

Kindness in Action: Can you think of a time when everything seemed to be going wrong and you were "hijacked" by your anger or frustration? (It happens to all of us.) What might you have done to derail the train that led you to act or speak in ways you later regretted? What would you like to do next time? Can you think of a time when you didn't feel the energy or inclination for kindness, but you did it anyway? How did that feel? Do you participate in gossip or saying things about others behind their backs that you would never say to their faces? Next time you realize such a conversation has begun, see how you can change the tone or close it gracefully.

Chapter 42:

Being Kind to People We Don't Like

"I have learned silence from the talkative, toleration from the intolerant, and kindness from the unkind." (Khalil Gibran)

Try as we might, there are very likely going to be people we just don't like and probably never will. I'm not talking about the crooks, criminals, and psychopaths whom we wisely disdain and avoid, but the everyday disagreeable creatures, nuisances, and curmudgeons who populate our lives and challenge us in unwelcome ways.

We encounter them occasionally—the ornery neighbor, the obstinate board member, the know-it-all acquaintance, the perpetually petulant client. Maybe they're even a relative. We can ignore them to the degree possible, but even then they're still present, a plaguing irritation that brings clouds to otherwise sunshiny days.

Radical Kindness

What if we engage in radical kindness? What if we not only tolerate our encounters with taxing people, but strive to see something in them that is likable and even admirable? What if we learn to feel gratitude for these people in our lives?

If we approach our encounters with the apparent irritants in our lives with a spirit of inquiry and openness, we may be surprised to learn that the everyday jerks we encounter have some pretty good qualities. We may also recognize that there are likely to be people who see us as the everyday jerks in their lives.

You've heard me say many times that I am a firm believer in the notion that what we look for is generally what we find. So those people who spend their days looking for things to criticize find them everywhere, and likewise, people who look for things to admire and appreciate find those in abundance.

What would happen if instead of avoiding or grudgingly accepting the annoying people in our lives—the ones we've never learned to like—we deliberately look for their kindness? Maybe that neighbor who complains about everything and yells at kids for making too much noise loves animals and takes care of wounded birds. And maybe his kindness is masked by shyness, fear, or social ineptitude. Maybe it's not evident on the surface, but if we look deeper, we're going to find it. Maybe that board or committee member who sets everyone's teeth on edge with her negativity and self-promotion does pro bono work in underserved communities. Or maybe we can appreciate her commitment to the organization, even if we struggle to appreciate her methods. What if, knowing that our path is going to cross with a person we have not been able to like, we determine that we will look for their kindness and find a way for their kindness and ours to intersect? It's all about going beyond merely gritting our teeth and tolerating a person to finding a way to recognize their best qualities and welcoming them into our lives.

I'm lucky that there are very few people in my life whom I dislike. Over the years, I've seen that people I may initially feel some aversion toward become quite likable once I get to know them. They didn't change; I did. Everything changes once I turn off that judgmental part of me and recognize that a behavior I find displeasing may be the result of fear, uncertainty, or clumsiness. We're all just doing the best we can, and for most of us, our best will always be imperfect, since we are a work in progress until the day we die.

Abraham Lincoln is quoted as having said, "I don't like that man. I must get to know him better." What wisdom and self-awareness! To overcome any dislike I may feel, I've been trying to look for the kindness in those few objectionable people I encounter. Kindness is there—in nearly everyone—and it's surprisingly easy to find. What I'm learning is that I am better able to separate the person from their behaviors, so that I am now able to say, "I appreciate that person, even if I don't like or understand some of their actions."

There are exceptions to every rule, and thus, there are bound to be some people who seem to defy all efforts to be seen as likable. I've finally learned that they're in our lives for a reason, too, and an important one. From them, we learn tolerance, or perhaps patience, or perhaps we recognize some quality of our own that in them is magnified to a degree that is instantly offensive. If nothing else, maybe we can appreciate them for their role as a warning to others not to behave this way. With these few individuals, our choice then becomes whether to let them negatively influence our behaviors and beliefs, or to look harder for their kindness, and to extend kindness as best we can and be grateful for what we have learned from them.

We never go wrong if we look for kindness.

Kindness in Action: *Are there people in your life whom you simply cannot like and in whom you can find no redeeming qualities? Perhaps the way they act offends you, or things they say are offensive. Perhaps their beliefs are so opposite your own that you can see nothing agreeable about them. Look a little bit harder. Is there something that you can accept and maybe even admire about them? Look at it another way: Might there be anything in their worst behavior that you fear you could also be guilty of—even if only at a microscopic level? Can you at least see them as a lesson in what you don't ever want to be? What lesson can you learn from them? Try to turn your dislike into curiosity, and then into sympathy or empathy.*

Chapter 43:

I'm Just Sayin' . . .

Honesty Isn't Always Kind

"Today I bent the truth to be kind, and I have no regret, for I am far surer of what is kind than I am of what is true."
(Robert Brault)

"I'm just saying this for your own good."

"Don't be so thin-skinned. I'm just telling it like it is."

"Hey, I call it like I see it."

"Jeez, you're so touchy!"

These phrases are often used to justify saying hurtful things. Sometimes the speaker may really believe that the listener needs to hear his unvarnished opinion about the poor sap's looks, abilities, opinions, or prospects.

Speaking on behalf of poor saps everywhere, we don't. We don't need someone to tell us all the things that are wrong with us or all the things we don't do as well as we should. That's what that persistent little voice in our own head does—and it doesn't need any help.

There are things that need to be said and things that don't need to be said. If we pause to think before we speak, we generally know the difference.

"You'd be so much prettier if you'd just lose fifteen pounds," doesn't need to be said—ever.

"You might want to get that spinach off your front tooth before you make your presentation," needs to be said. *And thank you!*

"The other kids in your class certainly have more artistic ability than you do," doesn't need to be said, even if it's abundantly clear to everyone but your eight-year-old that she'll never be a budding Monet.

I don't advocate lying. I was raised in a home where honesty was valued, and I consider honesty to be one of the most important characteristics of good people. That being said, I believe there are times when telling the truth may not be the best course of action. And being able to discern the appropriate time for truth-telling and the appropriate time for silence or even a judicious fib is another important characteristic of good people, certainly of kind ones.

Some lies are obvious, some a bit more subtle.

To the question, "Honey, does this dress make me look fat?" any spouse who answers with anything but, "You look gorgeous!" or a similarly reassuring exclamatory statement really hasn't thought through the business of being married.

"How delightful! Thank you for being so thoughtful!" in response to an ugly, impractical, or totally preposterous gift is always a wise response, even if it's a whopper of a lie. Would you really rather hurt the giver's feelings and then live with the regret of having done so? Receiving graciously—even when the gift is unwanted—is one of the kindest behaviors we can learn.

"I'm fine, thanks for asking." There are times—and we usually know when they are—when telling an acquaintance about our persistent rash, impending colonoscopy, or chronic foot fungus is entirely unnecessary. The depth of the relationship is a good gauge of how much detail to provide when someone asks the innocuous and automatic question, "How are you?"

Certainly there are times when we are not fine, when we are the furthest thing from fine, and when we need to share our pain with good and true friends. That's what friendship is all about. But people who are never fine, who always have a complaint—a woe or malady that they seemingly can't wait to share with anyone who will listen—become people others avoid. Then, ironically, they have something else to moan about.

If you're inclined to be a moaner, there's a simple trick to start changing that habit. Smile. That's it, smile. There's abundant research that smiling when we don't feel happy makes us happy. That smile may start out as a lie, but it becomes truth as we allow our mood to improve and we see the smiles of others returned to us.

If you're contemplating telling a lie, think about your motive behind it:

Are you lying to make yourself appear to be something that you are not—smarter, stronger, more successful, or more interesting? Think again, and exercise your courage muscles. You're fine exactly as you are—why pretend to be something that you're not? Would you rather be authentic or an imposter? Would you rather people liked and respected you for who you really are, or because they think you're something that you're not? Besides, when you deceive others, you must remember the story you fabricated—otherwise you are likely to get caught in your lie later—and you'll either feel foolish or have to come up with more lies. It's not worth it.

Are you lying to make a sale, deflect blame, get recognized, or advance your career? I can recall times when employees lied to cover up a mistake they had made. Or didn't admit a mistake in hopes that it would not be discovered. It always came to light later, and we scrambled to fix the problems that resulted from the cover-up. I can also recall many times when employees came to me to admit an error as soon as they realized it happened. I always thanked them for doing so. And I was genuinely grateful. It's been my experience that virtually anything is fixable if we know about it—and the sooner the better. We then worked together to come up with a solution, and often the solution strengthened the situation. My respect and trust for the employees who told the truth always grew, while trust and respect were diminished for employees who lied or covered up. No matter how innocuous the lie may seem, your trustworthiness and integrity are at stake here—even if you're the only one who knows that. Are they worth tarnishing for *anything*? I recently came upon a quote by Ryan Freitas that sums it up pretty well: "Your reputation is more important than your paycheck, and your integrity is worth more than your career."

Are you lying to spare someone's feelings? Under these circumstances, lying may be both acceptable and desirable. Add another question: Is anyone harmed? Is there a downside to telling my work colleague that her new hairstyle is great when, in fact, my first thought was that she looks like a radish on a stick? When I get used to it, I'll surely like it more.

Other questions to consider:

- If I were in his or her position, would I want the truth or a gentle lie?
- Which response best serves kindness: the truth, a considerate lie, or silence?

My sister and I still commiserate (it's cheaper than therapy) over our mother's "truth-telling" when we were children: to Kim that her mouth was too big and her smile showed too much of her teeth and gums—causing my sister for decades to cover her mouth when she smiled or laughed, rather than display her genuine delight; and to me that I could always have a nose job if my nose got any bigger. Until my mother mentioned it, I had been totally unaware that my proboscis was anything less than perfect. Thanks, Mom! Fortunately, my husband thinks my straight, Roman nose *is* beautiful.

My friend Nancy shared with me that one of the hospice caregivers who helped her family during her grandmother's final weeks used the phrase "a loving lie." This acknowledges that there are times when lying may be a necessity, when it's done with compassion and to ease someone's pain. Looked at in these terms, honesty—such a valued and important trait— cannot be an absolute.

Another consideration of whether to tell the truth or to dissemble is whether you can make a contribution to the outcome.

If your colleague has already gotten the haircut, or your spouse has already purchased and worn the loud Hawaiian shirt, then little is served by telling them what you really think. But if they ask you in advance how you think they would look with a radical 'do, or wearing a bright yellow shirt with orange-and-purple parrots, a diplomatic truth might help them make a different decision.

Similarly, we don't need to be the people who point out the typo, criticize the amount of cumin in the soup, or correct a stranger's mispronunciation. If someone asks for my input, I'll gladly give it—unless it appears that they really just want support and kudos—then I'll give those. I've found as I've gotten older that I've also gotten quieter. I don't need to point out somebody else's foibles and failures. I've got plenty of my own.

But my nose, fortunately, is quite perfect.

Kindness in Action: *Can you recall people telling you hurtful things "for your own good"? Are you still holding on to any of those criticisms and letting them nip at you like mosquitoes? Next time you hear that unkind voice, tell it firmly that you don't need its advice and to please not come around again. If someone's "truth-telling" still keeps you from doing something that you've always wanted to do, set a time right now to try it. What does it matter if you aren't great at it— the point is to overcome the limiting mindset and to have fun!*

Think about times when you've lied—has it been to gain something or to avoid admitting a mistake? Can you picture yourself in the same circumstance telling the truth instead? How does that feel? Next time you're in a similar circumstance, can you tell the truth?

Chapter 44:

When the Kindest Thing to Do Is . . .

Absolutely Nothing

"Don't underestimate the value of doing nothing, of just going along, listening to all the things you can't hear, and not bothering." (Winnie the Pooh)

As I wander around exploring kindness, I've been surprised to realize that quite often, choosing to do nothing is the kind choice. That probably flies in the face of any image we might have of the kindest people being ones in tights and a cape, with a big **K** emblazoned across their chest, leaving a trail of good deeds in their wake.

I suspect we've all witnessed or been involved in situations where feelings were hurt and tempers were raised as a result of emails that never should have been sent. That's one of the problems with email. It's just so enticing to reply immediately—in the heat of the moment—before we've really thought through what the sender may have intended, how our reply might be

interpreted—or misinterpreted—and what our ultimate goal
for the communication is.

Do we want to be right (or righteous), or do we want to
keep the peace? Sometimes, we can't do both, and we need to
decide which is more important.

I think there was probably a time in my life when being
right (or, I admit it, righteous) may have felt more important
than keeping the peace or being kind. Being right doesn't seem
all that important anymore. I'm reminded of a line from the
classic film *Harvey*, where Elwood P. Dowd, played to perfection
by Jimmy Stewart, says, "Years ago my mother used to say to
me . . . 'In this world, Elwood, you must be oh so smart or oh so
pleasant.' Well, for years I was smart. I recommend pleasant."

This harks back to something we talked about earlier:
the power of the pause. And the importance of delaying long
enough to decide if the action you're anticipating will really get
the results you want—results that are ultimately best for all. It's
the simple but frequently ignored recognition that knee-jerk
reactions often result in making us jerks. When we hit pause,
we may realize that we should make that pause permanent and
simply do nothing, say nothing.

"Silence is sometimes the best answer," the Dalai Lama
wisely said. It's harder than it sounds, though—especially in
verbal interactions. A derisive comment, sarcastic reply, or
feeble attempt at humor may come to my lips quickly and be
uttered before I realize how snarky it sounds. I'm learning to
bite my tongue, but it is not always easy.

Even if my words aren't snarky, does what I'm saying help?
Maybe somebody in my office brings up an idea that they think
is great, but there are ramifications that make it unworkable
or unwise. How I communicate that may mean the difference
between their continuing to search for good ideas and their
feeling deflated and put down. Sometimes, the right thing to
do or say may be nothing—to let them discover the flaw for
themselves or even find a way to make the seemingly unworkable work. Or maybe the best course is to talk through the issue
in hopes that they see the unsoundness, or that I can point it

out considerately. Either way, the hasty, reactive response ("No, that will never work!") is not the best choice.

I think back on the four questions Rotarians ask to decide whether and how to act or speak:

- Is it the truth?
- Is it fair to all concerned?
- Will it build goodwill and friendship?
- Will it be beneficial to all concerned?

If the answer to any is no, don't say it or do it. Such good advice, it bears repeating!

Wise and Kind Parenting

I am not a parent and know little about raising children. (Borrowing a favorite line from an old David Mamet movie, I've never really seen the point of them.) I have a few friends, though, whom I consider to be extraordinarily good parents, and it seems that the wisdom to do nothing, in the name of kindness, is something great parents learn. As kids grow, there are times when parents need to let them learn lessons—sometimes painful ones—on their own. If Mom or Dad always steps in and clears the path or fixes the problem, the child will never learn independence. I'm guessing that it's terribly difficult for parents to do nothing when they know the lesson their child must learn will be accompanied by pain or distress. And to compound that, the kids—seeking rescue—rarely recognize that the parents' choice to do nothing is exactly the right one. But the parents know that the pain is temporary, and the lesson will last a lifetime.

And here's the amazing part: these parents also know that there are other times when the exact right thing to do is to step in and help solve the problem or avert the pain, and they do that. How do they know the difference? That discernment, that wisdom, fills me with awe.

I suppose, though, that the same wisdom parents have of when to intervene and when not to is what good leaders and managers have with their team members.

It may be tempting at times to tell ourselves that we are choosing to do nothing out of kindness, when really our kindness is sorely needed, and we are being lazy or apathetic. Kindness requires both mindfulness and honesty. If we pay attention, we will know what's right, and we will respond . . . or not, accordingly. It's wise to remember that if kindness were always easy, there'd be a lot more of it. We can only use our best judgment and choose as our heart directs us.

When we think about kindness, we tend to think about action: doing the right thing, saying just the right words, extending a hand at just the right moment. Let's allow for the possibility that there are times when kindness means restraint and inaction.

Kindness in Action: Can you think of a time when you did or said something that, upon reflection, might have been better left undone or unsaid? Have you had a chance to practice the power of the pause? If not, look for opportunities to try pausing before you speak or act. Can you recall a time when your own parents chose to do nothing rather than "rescue" you or step in and help? Was it the right thing to do (even though you may not have thought so at the time)? If you are a parent—or expect to be one—think about times when it might be kinder overall to do nothing, as well as times when you absolutely want to step in and help your child.

II. Creating a Kinder World

Chapter 45:

A Transformation or an Evolution?

The Five Percent Plan

"Even if our efforts of attention seem for years to be producing no result, one day a light that is in exact proportion to them will flood the soul." (Simone Weil)

Have you ever been adopted by a stray cat? It prowls the porch for a few weeks; you put out some water and maybe a smidge of tuna, and before you know it, you're hand-feeding him chicken marengo from the dinner table and making him a bed on the best chair in the bedroom.

That's how kindness sneaks up on you. You start small, and pretty soon it's a habitual practice that has made a home in your life.

I'm a big believer in incremental change. Maybe that's because attempts to make lofty changes all at once have never worked for me. Whether it's exercise, writing, or keeping my office clean, an attempt to go from zero to sixty in one big leap always seems to result in failure.

After years of thwarted good intentions, I finally realized that if I start small—exercise for fifteen minutes, write for one half hour, clean one shelf of my bookcase—the resulting good feelings reinforce the action, and I want to do more. And pretty soon a new habit is ingrained.

Kindness works the same way. One can't go from being oblivious and self-absorbed to being Mother Teresa's more compassionate sister by simply saying, "From now on, I'm going to be a kind person." We have years of inattention and self-centeredness to overcome, not to mention the attendant fears of having our kindness rejected or "doing it wrong." But we can go out of our way to perform one small kindness each day, and perhaps after a couple of weeks, perform two, or engage in a large act of kindness. As we see how good it feels, we want to do more, and pretty soon we're approaching every encounter with the hope that there will be an opportunity to extend ourselves.

I don't think there's such a thing as a *small* kindness. A warm smile, a kind word, a door held, or a burden shared—all influence the receiver to pass it on or pay it forward. We have no way of knowing how far one kind action can reverberate.

On the other side of the spectrum, we can stop the reverberation of unkindness by absorbing an insult without retaliating, or hearing harsh words and not hurling them back. These small—but difficult—acts will help to slow the epidemic of unkindness. That's hard to do, especially when we are just itching to voice the clever retort that will put that person in his or her place. It helps to approach such encounters with a spirit of inquiry, to ask what might be motivating this person to act as he does, and what burden he might be carrying that has shortened his temper and brought out the Darth Vader in him. We don't even have to understand—it's enough to recognize that there might be more going on than we can see, and to give the benefit of the doubt.

Kindness—like playing the piano or becoming proficient at golf—requires practice. One way to instill the practice that will lead to proficiency is to set an intention of being 5 percent kinder—to ourselves and to others. Just 5 percent—or maybe

2 percent, or 10. Not a lot, but just enough to notice the difference it makes. Let that small incremental change take root and flower. After a while, and with steady practice, kindness becomes both intentional and instinctive—and that's when magic happens.

Think about it for a moment. What would you do differently if you were just 5 percent kinder? To yourself? To others? To the planet?

I love the quote from French philosopher Simone Weil that opened this chapter: "Even if our efforts of attention seem for years to be producing no result, one day a light that is in exact proportion to them will flood the soul." It reminds me that if I put in the time to effect change and remain confident of the outcome, there will come a day when the transformation I desire will manifest—perhaps surprising me in its intensity.

Like the stray cat who comes to stay, let kindness creep in. Feed it and make a bed for it. Before you know it, the light will flood your soul.

 Kindness in Action: *Can you think of areas in your life where change or skill development came to you, not like a bolt from the blue, but so gradually that one day you simply realized something big had happened without you ever having had to struggle for it? Can you think of a time when you chose not to retaliate or snap back when you felt insulted or attacked—and the result was an end to the conflict? What would you do differently if you were just 5 percent kinder to the people in your life—family, friends, even strangers? What could you do today to be 5 percent kinder to yourself?*

Chapter 46:

What We Want Most for Our Kids

"It's not our job to toughen our children up to face a cruel and heartless world. It's our job to raise children who will make the world a little less cruel and heartless." (L. R. Knost)

My mother frequently said that what she wanted most for her daughters was for us to be happy. I think she hoped that we'd figure out on our own how to do that, since it was a state she achieved only rarely, and she was therefore unlikely to show us the way.

She said it often enough that I did spend some time pondering happiness as I was growing up. I never equated happiness with wealth or accumulation. I had a pretty strong notion that happiness wasn't a goal in itself, but more the by-product of doing what I loved in the company of people I respected and cared about. College and career taught me that happiness resulted when I could explore new ideas, meet challenges, problem-solve, create satisfying results, and improve the world in some small way—again, in the company of good people.

The happiness I experienced during my year of living kindly further clarified for me what brings joy. For me—and research shows it to be true for others—the most direct route to happiness is kindness. When I experience kindness, I am happy. It really is as simple as that. If I extend a kindness, it makes me happy. If I am on the receiving end of kindness, it makes me happy. And if I witness kindness, or even read about it, it makes me happy.

Considerable research bears this out. In recent years, there have been numerous studies linking kindness and happiness. A study by researchers Kathryn E. Buchanan and Anat Bardi, published in the *Journal of Social Psychology*[1], concluded that performing acts of kindness resulted in increased life satisfaction. The "Social Capital Community Benchmark Survey"[2], overseen by researchers from Harvard University, indicates that those who gave contributions of time or money were 42 percent more likely to be happy than those who didn't.

Similarly, research[3] by Sonja Lyubomirsky, professor of psychology at the University of California, Riverside, shows that acts of kindness boost happiness. She cites a study that showed "when nine- to eleven-year-old kids were asked to do acts of kindness for several weeks, not only did they get happier over time but they became more popular with their peers." Another of her research projects[4] showed that asking employees to be generous to a randomly chosen list of colleagues increased happiness, connectedness, and optimum engagement, plus it decreased depression—not just for the givers but also for the recipients, and even for people who merely witnessed the generosity. Once again, the power of kindness knows no bounds!

It holds true for self-kindness, too. Stanford psychologist Emma Seppälä, PhD, author of *The Happiness Track*, reports, "Research shows that self-criticism is basically self-sabotage, whereas self-compassion—treating yourself with the understanding, mindfulness, and kindness with which you would treat a friend—leads to far greater resilience, productivity, and well-being."[5] So when we teach kids to be kind to others, we need to also teach them to have compassion for themselves.

I wish my mother had known all of this, but then I also realize that it's something each of us needs to discover for ourselves.

I came across an article[6] not too long ago that summarized a research study conducted by Forum Research at the behest of the *Toronto Star*. It asked parents and grandparents the most important values they hoped to instill in their children and grandchildren. Kindness, I am happy to report, was the number one value these folks hoped to pass on to children, with 30% of respondents rating kindness at the top. Number two was a good work ethic, at 25%. Much lower on the list were ambition (8%), leadership (7%), curiosity (5%), courage (5%), and teamwork (4%).

There is an inherent problem with polls such as this: none of these values exist alone. Kindness requires courage, and it also requires curiosity; a good work ethic goes hand in hand with leadership and teamwork. Asking people to choose one among such interconnected values is misleading. Nonetheless, I am pleased to see the recognition people have for the importance of kindness, and I hope that parents and grandparents will not only wish it for their kids but also model it.

How to Raise Kids to Be Kind

Adults who want their kids to learn kindness must realize that such instruction begins at home—in how they see their parents and grandparents treat one another, as well as how they treat friends, kids, strangers, animals, and even the earth. As James Baldwin said, "Children have never been very good at listening to their elders, but they have never failed to imitate them." They are also smart enough to recognize that a value not practiced consistently is not a value at all.

Kindness must be evident always, not just when it's easy. They need to see that their parents will be kind behind the wheel even when other drivers are behaving like motorized maniacs. They need to see kindness at a crowded sporting event when the beloved home team is taking a thorough drubbing.

And when one is conversing with someone whose views are diametrically opposed to their own. And even in the privacy of one's home when talking about a difficult neighbor, work colleague, or relative.

Harvard psychologist Richard Weissbourd, who directs the university's Making Caring Common project, identified five ways to raise children to truly value kindness[7]:

1. Show kids that caring is a priority. Adults need to assure that their own behaviors match the messages they tell their kids. They need to walk their talk.

2. Give kids opportunities to practice caring and helpfulness, and to express gratitude. Kindness is a learned behavior that will be strengthened with repeated opportunities to extend oneself and feel the satisfaction of helping. Kids who learn the habit of gratitude are more likely to be helpful, generous, compassionate, and forgiving, as well as happy and healthy.

3. Help kids broaden their perspective and their circle of caring. The study describes this as "zooming in" and "zooming out"—this means learning to recognize kindness opportunities in one's circle of friends and family, and also to see the bigger picture of the need for kindness with strangers, the community, and even on a vaster, global scale.

4. Provide strong moral role models. Here researchers stress the need for parents to acknowledge their own mistakes, and to listen to kids and help them understand the world and develop empathy.

5. Help kids manage destructive feelings. Feelings such as anger, shame, or envy are unavoidable—but they can be expressed in harmful ways or they can be instructive and constructive. Through conversation, reading, playing games, and watching movies together, parents can help kids navigate the normal emotional roller coaster of childhood and adolescence.

Helping children witness and experience kindness and then talking with them about kindness may be among the most potent of all parenting skills. It's the formula for raising kind and happy children . . . ones who ultimately will become kind and happy adults. The world needs them now and will surely need them later.

***Kindness in Action:** What were the messages you received from parents and teachers growing up? Were you encouraged to always be first, or to be a team player, or perhaps smart, clever, successful, happy, strong, kind? If kindness was encouraged, was it consistently modeled? If you have kids, plan to have kids, or otherwise have children in your life, what do you wish for them, and how can you encourage them to be kind? Are you a role model for a kind life? Make it a practice to talk to your kids about kindness—and remember that talking means listening! You'll learn a lot if you let them tell you their thoughts and experiences related to kindness.*

Chapter 47:

Kindness to the Earth and

All Its Creatures

"Humankind has not woven the web of life. We are but one thread within it. Whatever we do to the web, we do to ourselves. All things are bound together. All things connect." (Chief Seattle)

While my kindness focus has mostly been on interaction between and among humans, a kind life encompasses more than just our species. Kindness extends to the animals with whom we share the planet, and to the planet itself.

There are other people who are far more qualified than I to talk about the importance of respecting and protecting the earth, and about sustainability efforts that will ultimately serve us all and all the generations that (I am hopeful) will follow. But I do know that as each of us claims our kindness and commits to a kind life, we must decide for ourselves what that means in terms of our nonhuman interactions.

There are many people—often politicians and policy-makers—who deny an overwhelming body of evidence that our planet is in jeopardy, people who believe we can exploit the earth's resources endlessly without damage or consequence. And there are people who recognize the damage we're doing but are willing to overlook it for the short-term profit that accrues to them.

What's the kind response? Is it to call them idiots or portray them as ostriches with their heads in the sand? That further polarizes us. When we hold opposing positions on environmental or political issues and we attack those with alternate views—or are attacked by them—we tend to dig in our heels, resulting in more polarization. Those who are still neutral don't want to align with *either* side—zealots being exhausting companions.

Civil dialogue is essential. Dialogue that explores the issues, assesses evidence, examines options and outcomes, and respects disagreement. Dialogue where *we assume one another's good intent.* It's not going to work if participants engage in name-calling, hyperbole, or insolence, or if discussion itself is disallowed by authority, as we've seen in some places.

The first time I became aware of the fragility of our planet was when we spent some time discussing Rachel Carson's groundbreaking book *Silent Spring* in a sixth-grade science class. A few years later, in 1970, the first Earth Day was held to address rising concerns about air pollution, pesticide use, water quality, and endangered species. Nearly fifty years later, we face many of the same concerns. Some problems have improved, but many have become more complex and more dire. The world's population was 3.7 billion people in 1970; today it's nearly double that number. And we don't always tread lightly on our beleaguered planet.

That first Earth Day led to the creation of the United States Environmental Protection Agency and the passage of the Clean Air, Clean Water, and Endangered Species Acts. Those acts have achieved a lot. But not nearly enough.

On an individual level, millions of people have changed

their habits since 1970—we recycle, we avoid pesticides, we compost. It is making a difference. But it's discouraging to see that corporate pollution is often still happening, many policymakers still deny the problem, and many of our fellow humans just don't seem to care. Some scientists warn that we are approaching a tipping point—a point of no return—if we continue to pretend that it's not our problem and that human activities can't hurt our planet.

It feels like the ultimate unkindness to ignore the earth and allow our shortsightedness to damage the planet beyond repair and put our own species—as well as countless others—in jeopardy. If there's anything we owe the generations that follow us, it's a commitment to our planet's health and long-term viability.

At least part of the solution is to be found in kindness—acknowledging where there is disagreement and agreeing to seek solutions without name-calling, histrionics, or political posturing. If we adults cannot do it, let it be a children's crusade. On this subject, they seem to be far more rational and tolerant. Who better to educate adults about the consequences of their actions than those who will suffer or benefit from the decisions we make now?

Extending kindness to the earth needn't mean drastic actions or enormous changes to our lives. Largely, it's a matter of paying attention (as are most things). What can each of us do to protect and nurture the planet that protects and nurtures us? Here's what comes to my mind—what else can you think of?

- Sign up for a volunteer project—cleaning up a stream, planting trees, beautifying a park.
- Check with your waste management company to be sure you know everything you can recycle and how best to do it—those rules are frequently changing.
- Spend some time outdoors—walk along the beach, hike the hills, go to a park (and pick up any trash you encounter) . . . or just enjoy your backyard.

- Register with dmachoice.org or catalogchoice.org to reduce the unwanted catalogs you receive—it saves trees, and you won't be inundated with catalogs that insist you need stuff you really don't need.
- Think before you print out emails or unnecessary reports at work.
- Remember to bring your reusable bags when you shop.
- Plant a vegetable or herb garden.
- Look into composting if you aren't already doing it.
- Reduce or eliminate pesticide use in your garden.
- Plant a tree. Or two.
- Do some of your shopping at your local farmers market.
- Make a donation to an environmental cause you feel strongly about.
- Take shorter showers—or, better yet, shower or bathe with your sweetie.
- Ride a bike, walk, or use public transportation in place of driving when possible.

We don't have to do them all. Just pick one or two, and when they become habits, pick another couple. Everything we do or choose not to do—large or small—makes a difference.

Extending kindness to the earth is the same as extending it to our friends, our families, and ourselves. And while kindness is something we give with no other motive and no expectations of return, the kindness we offer our planet will come back to us tenfold: in clean, healthy air; clear and refreshing water; the shade of stately trees; and the bounty of our food. Like so many other things related to kindness, it only requires that we be mindful.

How we treat animals is another measure of our kindness. Sometimes it seems that it is easier to be kind to animals than to others of our own species. There was a story in our local paper about traffic being stopped in both directions on a busy street as a mother duck and her brood of ducklings leisurely crossed four lanes to safety. Drivers got out of their cars to direct traffic and protect the avian parade as commuters watched with patience and even delight. People didn't honk their horns; they didn't yell. I'm guessing all drove away from the scene with smiles on their faces, enchanted by the kindness they had just been witness to.

Would the drivers have been as patient if the traffic jam had been of human making? Hardly. There would have been honking, hollering, and certainly gritted teeth by the time traffic started moving again.

Yes, it's true that humans are not "dumb" animals and are accountable for their actions. Ducks are . . . well, they're ducks. And they're *cute*. A traffic jam of human making might be the result of stupidity, carelessness, or the sheer fact of too many humans—and their machines—in one place. That's just asking for trouble. Patience wears thin; judgments become harsh. We slip into unkindness.

Ducks are a different story entirely, as are puppies, kittens, and most animals, especially the babies of the species. Cute often trumps impatience, judginess, and even irritation.

Plus, it's less threatening to be kind to animals. When they reject our efforts, it doesn't jeopardize our self-worth. We recognize that they may be afraid or even injured. In the case of our animal companions, the unconditional love they offer is rarely matched by our human companions, and it is certainly less complex or fraught with misunderstanding.

Unfortunately, though, there are some people who are cruel to animals, even some who take pleasure in such cruelty. We are outraged when we hear of the brutality or neglect they inflict upon creatures. A friend recently described to me how she saw a driver deliberately swerve his car to hit a rabbit on the shoulder of a road. What makes someone do something like that? It baffles me.

If there are people who are cruel to animals and uniformly kind to people, I have not heard of them. Nor had Immanuel Kant, who said, "He who is cruel to animals becomes hard also in his dealings with men. We can judge the heart of a man by his treatment of animals."

I can remember a friend once telling me that she judged whether a man was worth dating a second time by how he treated her dog. She said that measure never steered her wrong.

Still, even if we are not *unkind* to animals, we can probably be kinder to them. For some, kindness to animals will extend to becoming vegetarians or vegans, or refusing to wear clothes made with fur or animal skins. Each of us must decide for ourselves what animal kindness means. Thinking about our place in the web of life and making our decisions based on thoughtful examination is an act of kindness. We must make these decisions for ourselves.

Some ideas that I have tried to apply to my life include:

Buying Humanely Raised Products

That means seeking out eggs, meat, and dairy products that are humanely raised, such as American Humane Certified™ products, helping to ensure the welfare of farm animals. Personally, I'm not ready to become a vegetarian—I like my husband's chicken marsala, and sometimes I crave a good hamburger—but I do want to be mindful about how my carnivorous habits impact the earth and its creatures.

Protecting Wild and Domestic Animals

Learn about conservation efforts and teach kids about wild animals and the need to protect them by visiting parks, accredited zoos, and aquariums. These are not simple issues—they are socioeconomic and cultural, and hugely complex. Education is one good place to start. Show by your words and your example that pets are to be treated with kindness, respected, and protected.

Adopting from Animal Shelters

If you are seeking a pet, adopt or rescue one from an animal shelter, thus saving the life of one of the six to eight million animals who end up abandoned each year. They are so cute, you'll probably want two.

If you have kids, there's no better place to start deepening everyone's connection to animals. Bonding with them to care for the creatures that enrich our lives so greatly and ask so little of us in return brings abundant joy. Take a moment to hug your dog or your cat, or to appreciate the birds in your trees or the squirrels in your yard. How empty our world would be without them!

Kindness in Action: *Take a walk in a favorite spot in nature and think about what kindness to the planet means to you. Review some of the suggestions above and add some ideas of your own. What can you commit to this week that will start making a difference in protecting the earth? Once that practice is habitual or easy, add another. Be especially mindful of how you interact with animals—whether pets, wild animals, or those we consume as food. If you are a meat or fish eater, commit to supporting only responsibly and humanely raised animals. Also, take a lesson from Native American and other cultures and express your gratitude to the creatures whose lives sustain your own. These are wonderful conversations to have with children; be sure to listen as much as you speak—or more. You will be surprised and touched by their wisdom. Remember that we are leaving the earth and its stewardship to them.*

Chapter 48:

Strategies for Bringing Kindness

into Your Life

"If the world seems cold to you, kindle fires to warm it."
(Lucy Larcom)

Choosing to live a life of kindness requires that we become activists in our own lives in a variety of ways. We need to take initiative to extend kindness—even if we don't feel like it. We need to speak up when we see unkindness or injustice. We need to look for opportunities to be kind and recognize kindness when we witness it. Contrary to the old adage, kindness is not necessarily one of the good things that come to those who wait. We need to actively pursue it.

There are ways we can bring more kindness into our lives. Juliana Breines, PhD, a postdoctoral fellow at Brandeis University, wrote an article entitled "Three Strategies for Bringing More Kindness into Your Life"[1] for UC Berkeley's Greater Good Science Center.

She describes ten core kindness practices, under three broad categories, that research shows will enhance kindness and generosity, leading to increased overall satisfaction with life.

Cultivating Feelings of Kindness

The first category of kindness practices deals with cultivating feelings of kindness. For each of the painless strategies enumerated, there are research studies showing their effectiveness in enhancing our desires to be kind and compassionate.

Feeling Connected Practice: This practice asks us to think about a time when we felt strongly connected to another person—perhaps by a shared experience or a profound conversation. Research has shown that this simple exercise increases concern for others and spurs intentions to perform generous acts. The explanation for this outcome, according to Breines, is "feeling connected to others satisfies a fundamental psychological need to belong; when this need is unmet, people are more likely to focus on their own needs rather than caring for others."

Feeling Supported Practice: Another simple practice, this one involves thinking about a time when you were comforted or supported by others, and the qualities and actions of those people who supported you. Research has shown that this practice increases our compassion and willingness to assist a person in need or in distress. In addition to instilling a feeling of "attachment security," this practice reminds us of the qualities we want to exhibit in ourselves.

Take an Awe Walk: I love this one. An awe walk is a stroll to a place that makes us feel "connected to something greater than ourselves." It might be the ocean, a forest, or whatever to us seems immense and "perspective-shifting." For each of us, that awe walk may be a different destination—it could be a lengthy hike or a few steps from our back door.

Compassion Meditation Practice: This is often referred to as lovingkindness meditation. It's a practice combining breathing with extending feelings of goodwill toward oneself, one's loved ones, acquaintances and strangers, and even people we dislike (we've also talked about this in Chapter 24). Breines cites research that just two weeks of compassion meditation results in more generous behaviors and even alteration in the parts of our brains that govern compassion and emotional responses. You can find many guides to compassion meditation online.

Increasing the Happiness We Get from Kindness

This next set of strategies deals with ways to be more intentional about practicing kindness in our own lives—and turning kindness into a habit. If you want to increase the number of kind and generous acts you perform, try these proven practices:

Random Acts of Kindness: Such acts are usually simple, spontaneous actions, such as picking up the tab for a stranger's coffee, putting money in the meter so someone doesn't get a ticket, or donating blood. This practice suggests performing five random acts in a single day and then writing about the experience. Breines notes that performing random acts of kindness both lifts our spirits and increases our self-esteem.

Making Giving Feel Good: There's a difference between giving because we feel pressured or obligated to do so and giving because we want to.

The former may not feel good and may even lead to resentment. The latter does feel good and increases our personal satisfaction. To avoid the negative feelings, we need to make giving a choice; whether we are being asked to give or asking others to give, it must be okay to say no. An additional way to make giving feel good is to make a connection with the recipient of your kindness—don't just hand a homeless person a couple of dollars and hurry on; take a moment to make eye contact and exchange a few kind words—it's easy, and it will make you both feel good. Another is to learn about the impact of your generosity—if you give time or money to a cause, take time to learn about how people are positively impacted by your generosity.

Inspiring Kindness in Others

The next set of practices contains ways to help others see the value of kindness and engage in kind actions.

Reminders of Connectedness: This is simply examining our surroundings and looking for ways to create reminders of the importance of kindness and connectedness. It might be pictures of people working together placed on the walls of a classroom, posting on an office bulletin board letters of thanks from constituents who were helped by our work, or an inspiring quotation at the top of a board meeting agenda. Look around your place of work for spaces to convey your team's connectedness or your shared mission.

Putting a Face on Human Suffering: Sometime kindness requires a kick in the pants—to help us overcome that powerful inertia that keeps us from acting. Sharing pictures or stories of people in need often lights a fire of action and involvement—motivating people to help. A photo or story can motivate more people to action more effectively than faceless reams of data. We've seen many times that a photograph of an abandoned dog or cat in a cage at the humane society spurs the adoption of stray animals far better than reports citing the statistics of homeless animals.

Shared Identity: This practice asks us to explore ways of forging a sense of our common humanity across group boundaries. Whether it is our common love for our children or mutual passion for a sport, we can overcome fear and mistrust by developing a sense of shared affinity. When we take time to think about it, we have so many more similarities than differences with people who may seem alien to us.

Encouraging Kindness in Kids: If we can instill kindness at an early age, we can change the world. Strategies for nurturing children's natural propensity toward kindness and generosity include avoiding external rewards for kind behavior so kids see that kindness is its own reward; praising kids' character so they come to see themselves as kind; when criticism is called for, criticizing the child's behavior, not their character; and modeling kindness ourselves.

As I review this list of strategies and behaviors that promote kindness, I'm struck by the fact that none of them are difficult; they simply require practice. Like anything we want to do well—from public speaking, to Ping-Pong, to piano playing—we get good at it by practicing. I can't think of anything more worthwhile to practice than kindness. Can you?

Kindness in Action: *What or where is your awe walk? Think about trying some of the above practices and incorporating them into your family or your business. Don't overwhelm yourself by trying everything at once—pick one for this week and then another for next week, and a third for the week after. For now, schedule an awe walk, or think about when you feel connected or supported; look into the lovingkindness meditation practice. Remember that kindness starts with being kind to yourself—and sometimes that's the hardest thing of all!*

III. Living Kindness Every Day:
Your Kindness Legacy

Chapter 49:

Kind Actions That Cost Nothing and Take Little Time

"You can't live a perfect day without doing something for someone who will never be able to repay you." (John Wooden)

A large element of kindness is giving—perhaps money, perhaps time. And being able to give without thoughts of getting something in return is certainly essential to a kind life. However, there may be times when neither time nor money is available to us. Does that mean we cannot still be generous . . . or kind?

Au contraire! We can always be kind. There are countless ways to be kind that don't require investments of time or money. They are not without some effort, though. Here are a few that come to mind. Some are self-explanatory, such as:

- We can make eye contact, smile, and say "good morning."
- We can say "thank you" or "I'm sorry."
- We can hold a door or offer help in carrying a heavy load.

- We can let the car merge in front of us.
- We can say something nice about an absent friend when others are gossiping about her.
- We can load the dishwasher, even if they aren't our dirty dishes (and unload it when the dishes are clean).
- We can acknowledge our own imperfections and over-look the foibles of others.

Other little-time/no-cost expressions of kindness invite us to delve deeper into their meaning:

If we can give nothing else, we can always give the benefit of the doubt. Rather than assume the worst, let the stories we make up about people or things we don't know be positive and affirming. We can assume one another's good intent—and life will be more enjoyable and more rewarding if we do.

We can let go of anger or resentment. We can forgive. Carrying around anger and resentment toward others, or regrets and recriminations toward ourselves, serves no one. Kindness happens when we learn from mistakes, slights, and injuries; forgive and open up to a new story.

We can listen for the music rather than the missed note. We've talked about the people who spend their time looking for the typo, catching others' errors, and playing "gotcha" with life. While sometimes that might be our day job if we're an editor, diagnostician, accountant, building inspec-tor, or the like, it needn't be our personal mission. The rest of the time, we can practice looking for what's right and letting go of the rest. Learning to let go is one of the great lessons of kindness—or, for that matter, of life. One of the best things we can learn is when something needs to be said and when it doesn't.

Kind words are powerful and always welcome.
We can compliment someone on the great service they provided, their perspicacity, a well-written report, or how their smile brightens a room. It's rare that we can't find something kind to say.

We can pay attention and express apprecia-tion for all that we notice. Paying attention to our lives is one of the secrets to a consistently kind life. If we are unaware of what's going on around us, it's so easy to miss opportunities to be kind, or miss the kindnesses extended to us by others. Opportunities to express kindness are all around us, but they're also easy to overlook if we aren't paying attention.

Of course, there are still many kindnesses that ask us to open not just our hearts but also our wallets, and ask us to commit our time as well as our intentions. It's rarely an either/or. When our hearts are open, we will do what we can, recognizing that we offer the best of who we are when we choose kindness.

Kindness in Action: For the next couple of days, notice all the opportunities you have to extend kindness and do so whenever possible. Notice, also, the responses you get from others—the smiles in return, the kind words, the acknowl-edgment. How does it feel if you overlook a perceived slight or choose not to say the critical remark to your family member or colleague? Little things can make a big difference. What's the very next little thing you can do to express your commitment to kindness?

Chapter 50:

A Dozen Reasons to Choose Kindness

"Kindness is more important than wisdom, and the recognition of this is the beginning of wisdom." (Theodore Isaac Rubin)

The decision to make kindness a central element in our lives does not automatically imbue us with that important quality. Like so many other things we choose to care about, that's just the beginning. Practice is required if we want to become proficient. Just as they say you need to practice if you want to play the piano well, or you need to write regularly if you want to be an author, or you need to keep perfecting your swing if you want to shoot par in golf, you also need to strengthen your kindness muscle by using it regularly. The result—eventually—will be that kindness comes naturally and even sometimes effortlessly. That's the sweet spot.

But, of course, if we're going to practice something, there needs to be a good reason. If it's writing, maybe you want to be published, or you want to be able to express yourself through stories that will entertain or inspire. If it's piano, maybe you want to connect with the music, be part of a jazz combo, or entertain friends. If it's golf, well, you're probably something of a masochist.

With regard to kindness, it should be enough just to know it's the right thing to do, but there are also many really good reasons to choose kindness and to practice it until it becomes ingrained in our reflexes. We've talked about them all, but as we approach our final chapters, it's worthwhile to remind ourselves what those reasons are:

1. Kindness is good for our health. There have been numerous studies about the health benefits of kindness. They show that people who are routinely kind get relief from chronic pain, stress, and insomnia, and they also have increases in happiness, optimism, and self-worth. More specifically:

2. Kindness has a positive effect on the body's immune system, as well as on the production of serotonin in the brain. Serotonin is a chemical created by the human body that has a calming, anti-anxiety effect.

3. Kindness is good for your heart. Acts of kindness often generate an emotional warmth, which produces the hormone oxytocin in the brain and body, which, in turn, releases nitric oxide in blood vessels causing them to dilate and lower one's blood pressure, acting as a cardioprotective agent. Oxytocin also reduces levels of free radicals and inflammation in the cardiovascular system, thus reducing heart disease.

4. Kindness slows aging. That same reduction of free radicals and inflammation slows aging in the human body. Compassion has similarly been linked to activity in the vagus nerve, which also regulates heart rate and controls inflammation levels in the body.

5. Kindness makes us happier. Kindness elevates the levels of dopamine in the brain, giving us a "natural high." It has been shown to substantially increase happiness and reduce depression.

6. Kindness improves relationships. Connecting with one another is actually a genetic predisposition, so kindness helps us build new relationships and enhance existing ones. If we want to bond with others and have deep connections in our lives, kindness is key.

7. Kindness is contagious. Just as the measles and the flu are contagious in a bad way, so is kindness in a good way. Kindness begets more kindness. When we're kind, we inspire kind behavior in others, and the effect ripples out beyond our awareness. Whether we extend kindness, receive kindness, or merely witness kindness, the result is the same: it acts as a catalyst for more kindness.

8. Kindness alleviates social anxiety. Research shows that engaging in acts of kindness reduces levels of social anxiety and social avoidance. Individuals who perform acts of kindness report lower levels of discomfort and anxiety about social interaction, and are more able to participate in group activities. We develop confidence through our kindness.

9. Kindness is a good reason to get ample rest and sleep. It's been shown that sleep helps us be kinder[1]. So getting your *zzzz*s is a way of extending kindness toward yourself and the planet. You don't need an excuse for that afternoon siesta! In addition, extending kindness when we're tired can be as replenishing as a catnap or a jolt of java.

10. Kindness has been linked to greater life satisfaction. Those who regularly extend generosity and perform acts of kindness report higher degrees of satisfaction with their lives.

11. Kindness makes the workplace more pro-ductive, profitable, and enjoyable. A kind work environment helps employees feel more engaged; it improves morale, builds loyalty and engagement, reduces absences, and increases profits. Forget all those old-school books on winning through intim-idation and fear; kindness is a better business model.

12. Kindness serves life. Kindness guides us to look for the positive rather than the negative, to seek the best in the people we encounter, and to embrace abundance: we *have* enough and we *are* enough. When we do these things, we offer our best selves to life and help manifest the world as we want it to be.

We don't really need reasons to extend kindness—kind-ness is simply the best expression of who and what we are. But in the face of myriad deadlines and obligations it's easy to look for shortcuts and overlook opportunities to extend kindness, so it never hurts to remind ourselves that there are really good reasons to be kind. And to practice kindness daily.

Kindness in Action: Do any of the reasons above partic-ularly resonate with you, such as the health effects of kindness, improved relationships, or perhaps business success? What do you see as the best reason for choosing kindness? Think about what you might do to create a frequent reminder not only to be kind but to be aware of how kindness is changing your life. (Remember, change often comes so gradually we don't even notice it until we suddenly recognize that a major shift has somehow occurred.) Are there friends, family members, or business associates you can talk to about your commitment to kindness—and invite them to join you on the journey?

Chapter 51:

The Lessons of Kindness

"It's all a matter of paying attention, being awake in the present moment, and not expecting a huge payoff. The magic in this world seems to work in whispers and small kindnesses." (Charles de Lint)

I encountered so many lessons during my year of living kindly—and I still chance upon them almost daily. Some are big and bold lessons, some subtle and hidden, more like quiet *aha*s that tap me on the shoulder or whisper in my ear. The more I look at those less obvious lessons, though, I see that there really are no small kindness lessons, just as there are no small kindnesses.

We never know how far our kindness will reverberate. Will the smile we extended to the bus driver cause him to greet each passenger with a kind word, and will each of those people, in turn, extend a kindness that they otherwise might not have, and will one of those kindnesses—or a further kindness—mend a heart, lift someone from despair, or even save a life?

No, there are no small kindnesses. And likewise, the

lessons of kindness may seem small, but they could extend far beyond our imagining.

Summarizing some of those quiet, aha lessons:

- Being kind and being nice are not the same thing. They're not.
- It takes patience to be kind and kindness to be patient.
- Curiosity can lead us to kindness. If we look for what's behind unkindness, we will often reach a place of understanding.
- Kindness is an evolution, not a sudden transformation. Like most of the best things in life, developing a life of kindness is a gradual process. Kindness is a path that is its own destination.
- Being able to accept kindness is as important as being able to extend kindness.
- Kindness begins with me. A life of kindness begins with self-kindness. If I don't think I'm worthy of my own kindness, how can I be consistently kind to others?
- Sometimes the kind thing to do is nothing . . . and that's not always easy.
- There's no such thing as selective kindness. The person who is kind to you but unkind to the waiter is not a kind person.
- Kindness and gratitude go hand in hand.
- I can take kindness seriously without taking myself too seriously.
- Like all things that we want to become good at, kindness takes practice.
- We teach kindness by modeling it, not by lecturing about it.
- The kinder we are, the more kindness we experience.
- Kind people are not without occasional bouts of pettiness, envy, anger, or impatience, but they are able to rise above their impulses and express kindness.
- If I am unable to see a way to express kindness I need to look more closely or broaden my field of vision.

All of these little *aha*s comprise a recipe for a kind life. None are terribly difficult, though practice is essential. If we can keep them in our hearts and in our awareness, we can not only enjoy a feast of compassion and connection, we can change the world.

My Biggest Kindness Lessons

While many of my kindness lessons came to me as quiet whispers, others whumped me upside the head—often multiple times—or bellowed to me from the treetops. These *eureka!* lessons are daily reminders of not only what it means to live a kind life but also what a difference a kind life can make. Here are my biggest lessons in kindness:

> **Pay attention:** A huge *aha!* is the role of mindfulness in kindness. All I need to do is pay attention, and I see that opportunities to extend kindness are everywhere, as are instances of kindness. So often, we operate on automatic pilot, oblivious to the people and circumstances around us, and the difference a word, a smile, or an act of kindness could make. I've come to see that the simple reminder to "pay attention" may be one of the universal secrets to a good life. And like so many other things related to kindness, it's simple, but it isn't easy. If we're present for our lives—paying attention, being "kindful"—we're going to recognize when our gifts are needed: a smile, a word of kindness, a proffered hand.

> **Pause:** I have likened the power of the pause to that of the Hoover Dam. It's that immense. Instead of speaking or acting in instant response to a situation, taking the time to pause and think about what I want my response to activate—and why—has been transformative. In the space of that brief pause, I might

totally change my reaction or perhaps decide not to respond at all. That pause has *always* guided me to a better place.

Let go of judgment: It's so easy when we see people behaving inconsiderately to judge them—especially in settings where we are thrown together to navigate crowded spaces, such as congested streets and highways or teeming markets and airports. In such settings, it often seems that strangers are there just to get in our way or slow us down. We judge them for their aberrant driving, for being oblivious obstructions, and sometimes just for taking up too much space on the planet. We do it to strangers, and often we do it to friends and loved ones, too—especially when we're feeling tired or depleted (while we tend to give ourselves a "pass" for similar behaviors!). Instead of attributing a silence or an ill-chosen word to malice or resentment, we can assume good intent. We can just as easily say to ourselves, "I'm sure she didn't mean that the way it sounded." Why wouldn't we want to believe the best rather than the worst? Suspending judgment is hard, but it's one of the first big steps in behaving kindly.

Kindness has no ending: It just keeps reverberating outward and serving life in ways we may never know. Every once in a while, you hear a story about someone who was at the end of their tether—about to explode or self-destruct—and an unexpected kindness arrived to diminish the pain and show them a more positive alternative. We can never know if even the tiniest kindness we extend might ripple out to eventually change the world. What a great reason to send out all the ripples we can and trust that we are making a difference!

Being kind is more important than being right: Another transformative *aha!* So many of us were raised to be smart—and rewarded for being smart—that we have often tended to value being smart over kind, and being right over . . . well, just about anything. It's not that we can't be both kind *and* smart or kind *and* right, but on those occasions when we have to choose between them, choosing kind is also our path to peace.

What we think about is what we become: And what we look for is what we are most likely to find. We can spend our time pursuing life's broken bits and catching others' mistakes, and the more we do it, the better we'll get at it. But where's the satisfaction in always playing "gotcha," and who will want to play with us? If we invest that energy, instead, in looking for what's right and what's good, and recognizing the special qualities of the people we encounter, life will be richer in every way. If we look for goodness and for kindness, we'll find them.

Kindness requires courage: Fear is probably the biggest reason we don't extend kindness. We fear rejection, being judged, looking foolish, or becoming vulnerable. We fear venturing into unexplored territory and being seen as weak or clumsy. Sometimes these fears are paralyzing. But the more we tap into and exercise our courage in the face of those fears, the less power they will have over us. Our courage grows the more we use it.

We can always choose kindness: We have control over both our perceptions and our reactions. We can choose the path that leads us to peace. It takes practice, but it's within our capabilities.

Kindness isn't a destination, it's a path: Kindness isn't something that I can adopt for a single year and then move on. My number one job is kindness. That's what I'm here for. So a year of living kindly becomes a commitment to living kindly. There will be slips, there will be stumbles, but after each I will get back on the path and keep moving forward—optimistically and with many people at my side. I hope you will be one of them.

These certainly aren't all the lessons of kindness. But over my year of trying to live a kind life, these were consistent and recurring themes. It seems to me that the most important lessons in life are ones that we learn, and relearn, and learn some more. I hope to go on learning these lessons . . . kindness still has much to teach me.

Kindness in Action: Do any of these insights resonate for you? Where do you see them in your life, and how can you stay connected to them? Are you ready to pay attention, claim your courage, suspend judgment, and choose kindness? Remind yourself throughout each day that you carry within you the power to change the world, and each time you exercise that power you are serving what's best in you and what's best in the world. Take some time to make a list of some of your own ahas related to kindness. Carry a copy with you for a couple of weeks and look at it periodically throughout the day. See if having these reminders in front of you helps you to choose kindness as opportunities arise, and to recognize kindness when you witness it. If we nurture it, the practice of kindness will become a habit that changes our lives.

Chapter 52:

The Never-Ending Dance:

A Kindness Manifesto

"No act of kindness, no matter how small, is ever wasted."
(Aesop)

By now, I hope you have claimed the label "kind" as your own. Maybe you're not *always* kind in *every* circumstance, and maybe you still fail to notice some opportunities to offer kindness. Perfection is not our aim here. You are, nonetheless, kind, and with each act of kindness you perform and each unkindness that you choose not to be provoked by, you are making a kinder world. You are in service to life. There can be no greater purpose.

In claiming kindness, you demonstrate a strength—a superpower—that some have yet to recognize. You need neither cape nor tights to exercise your power—you simply need to pay attention.

As you've read this book, you've assembled a sizable toolbox filled with a wide variety of tools to help you extend kindness, receive kindness, and even stop unkindness in its tracks. You know when to employ each tool to best result, and you know that practice will keep them—and you—sharp and ready. As needed in the service of kindness—which, really, is service to the world—you can call on patience, curiosity, courage, or a multitude of other qualities that support kindness.

If the toolbox analogy doesn't resonate for you, find one that does. How about thinking of kindness skills as apps you have downloaded for use as you need them? In your brain, you can easily click on gratitude, mindfulness, pause, or whatever app is most suitable for the situation.

I've found it helpful to create a "kindness manifesto" to guide me and remind me of my most important purpose. Feel free to adopt it as your own or, better yet, adapt it to express your own kindness declaration.

Kindness Manifesto

Pay attention. Remember that your intention will direct your attention. Choose to see goodness and kindness.

Withhold judgment. We can never know what challenges others are facing. The benefit of the doubt is one of the greatest gifts you can give.

Pause. You don't need to respond instantly. Think about the kind response, which is often silence.

Receive graciously. Kindness means receiving as well as giving. Understand the joy others feel in giving, and help them experience that joy.

Take care of you. Kindness begins with self. If we cannot be kind to ourselves, we have little to offer others. Accept your shortcomings, forgive your blunders, hold to your boundaries, and indulge in simple pleasures.

Be grateful. Kindness grows from a sense of abundance and appreciation. There is always something to be grateful for.

Every kindness matters, even the smallest. We never know how far our smile or kind word will ripple, so use every opportunity to create a ripple.

Choose peace. Life is not always easy and not always fair. Regardless, you can choose peace.

If kindness isn't evident, look harder. If you still can't see it, make it yourself.

Always choose kindness. You will never regret it.

Thank you for being part of the kindness community.

Together, we will change the world.

Notes

Chapter 5. Perform Two Acts of Kindness and Call Me in the Morning

1. Danica Collins, "The Act of Kindness and Its Positive Health Benefits," *Underground Health Reporter*, http://undergroundhealthreporter.com/act-of-kindness/.
2. David R. Hamilton, "5 Beneficial Side Effects of Kindness," *Huffington Post*, updated August 2, 2011, http://www.huffingtonpost.com/david-r-hamilton-phd/kindness-benefits_b_869537.html%20.
3. "Empathy Heals," *Scientific American Mind*, November 1, 2009, https://www.scientificamerican.com/article/nice-doctors-heal-faster/.
4. David Haslam, "The Best Health Care Must Involve Kindness and Instil Trust," *Huffington Post*, updated May 2, 2017, http://www.huffingtonpost.co.uk/david-haslam/the-best-healthcare-must-_b_9210460.html.
5. James R. Doty, "Why Kindness Heals," *Huffington Post*, updated January 26, 2017, https://www.huffingtonpost.com/james-r-doty-md/why-kindness-heals_b_9082134.html.

6. Jeffrey B. Young, "How the Power of Physician Empathy Helps Patients Heal Faster," *Dignity Health,* January 26, 2016, https://www.dignityhealth.org/articles/how-the-power-of-physician-empathy-helps-patients-heal-faster.
7. Conboy et al., "Which Patients Improve: Characteristics Increasing Sensitivity to a Supportive Patient-Practitioner Relationship," *Social Science & Medicine* 70, no. 3 (February 2010): 479–84, https://doi.org/10.1016/j.socscimed.2009.10.024.
8. Moira A. Stewart, "Effective Physician-Patient Communication and Health Outcomes: A Review," *Canadian Medical Association Journal* 152, no. 9 (May 1995): 1423–33.
9. Kevork Hopayian and Caitlin Notley, "A Systematic Review of Low Back Pain and Sciatica Patients' Expectations and Experiences of Health Care," *Spine Journal* 14, no. 8 (April 2014), http://dx.doi.org/10.1016/j.spinee.2014.02.029.

Chapter 6. Bibbidi-Bobbidi-Boo: Kindness Alleviates Social Anxiety

1. "What Is Social Anxiety?" *Social Anxiety Institute*, https://socialanxietyinstitute.org/.
2. Jennifer L. Trew and Lynn E. Alden, "Kindness Reduces Avoidance Goals in Socially Anxious Individuals," *Motivation and Emotion* 39, no. 6 (December 2015): 892–907, https://doi.org/10.1007/s11031-015-9499-5.

Chapter 7. An Epidemic of Our Own Choosing

1. Trevor Foulk, Andrew Woolum, and Amir Erez, "Catching Rudeness Is Like Catching a Cold: The Contagion Effects of Low-Intensity Negative Behaviors," *Journal of Applied Psychology* 101, no. 1 (January 2016): 50–67, https://doi.org/10.1037/apl0000037.
2. Trevor Foulk, quoted in "'Rudeness Is Contagious': How Your Attitude Could Hurt Your Co-workers," Lisa Flam, *Today*, https://www.today.com/health/rudeness-contagious-how-your-attitude-could-hurt-your-co-workers-t32731.

3. Barbara Mitchell, quoted in "Workplace Rudeness Is Highly Contagious, Study Says," Rob Stott, *Associations Now*, August 21, 2015, http://associationsnow.com/2015/08/study-finds-workplace-rudeness-highly-contagious/.

Chapter 8. The Business Case for Kindness

1. David K. Williams, "Nice Companies Really Do Finish First," *Forbes*, May 31, 2016, http://www.forbes.com/sites/davidkwilliams/2016/05/31/nice-companies-really-do-finish-first/#5afc74df3741.
2. Emma M. Seppälä, "The Unexpected Benefits of Compassion for Business," *Psychology Today*, April 22, 2013, https://www.psychologytoday.com/blog/feeling-it/201304/the-unexpected-benefits-compassion-business.
3. Kim Cameron and Lynn Wooten, "Leading Positively—Strategies for Extraordinary Performance," University of Michigan Center for Positive Organizations, http://positiveorgs.bus.umich.edu/wp-content/uploads/Glance-Leading-Positively.pdf.

Chapter 10. Kindness Means Suspending Judgment

1. Stephen R. Covey, *The 7 Habits of Highly Effective People*, anniversary ed. (New York: Simon & Schuster, 2013), 38.

Chapter 19. On the Receiving End of Kindness

1. Sarah L. Kaufman, *The Art of Grace: On Moving Well Through Life* (New York: W. W. Norton & Company, 2016), 278.
2. Dale Turner, *Imperfect Alternatives: Spiritual Insights for Confronting the Controversial and the Personal* (Homewood, IL: High Tide Press, 2005), 85.

Chapter 20. It All Starts with Kindness to Self

1. Faith Popcorn, *The Popcorn Report: Faith Popcorn on the Future of Your Company, Your World, Your Life* (New York: HarperCollins, 1991), 39.

Chapter 21. No Kindness Is Ever Too Small

1. "TNTs—Adrian Webster for London Business Forum," YouTube video, 2:11, posted by Lawrence Hunt on December 19, 2013, https://www.youtube.com/watch?v= dSd31NwyS24.
2. Mary Rowe, "Micro-affirmations & Micro-inequities," *Journal of the International Ombudsman Association* 1, no. 1 (March 2008), https://ombud.mit.edu/sites/default/files/documents/micro-affirm-ineq.pdf.

Chapter 22. Kindness and Abundance: Enough Is Enough!

1. Jennifer James, *Success Is the Quality of Your Journey* (New York: Newmarket Press, 1986).

Chapter 23. Gratitude Is a Companion to Kindness

1. Rachel Naomi Remen, "Growing New Eyes: The 3 Question Journal," http://www.rachelremen.com/growing-new-eyes/.

Chapter 24. Kindness and Generosity: It's Not All about Money

1. Sharon Salzberg, *The Kindness Handbook: A Practical Companion* (Boulder, CO: Sounds True, 2008), 21-22.

Chapter 25. Pay Attention: Kindness Requires Presence

1. "What Is Mindfulness?" *Greater Good*, http://greatergood.berkeley.edu/topic/mindfulness/definition.
2. Emiliana R. Simon-Thomas, "Meditation Makes Us Act with Compassion," *Greater Good*, April 11, 2013, http://greatergood.berkeley.edu/article/item/meditation_causes_compassionate_action.

Chapter 27. A Life of Kindness Requires Courage

1. Sandra Ford Walston, "Kindness Requires Courage," two-part interview by the author, September 1, 2015, https://ayearoflivingkindly.com/2015/09/09/kindness-requires-courage-an-interview-with-sandra-ford-walston/; https://ayearoflivingkindly.com/2015/09/16/kindness-requires-courage-part-2-of-an-interview-with-sandra-ford-walston/.

Chapter 28. Kindness and Curiosity

1. Ruth Henderson, "Kindness and Curiosity in Coaching," *Huffington Post,* updated June 30, 2015, http://www.huffingtonpost.com/ellevate/kindness-and-curiosity-in-coaching_b_7181190.html.
2. Emma Seppälä, "Why Compassion Is a Better Managerial Tactic than Toughness," *Harvard Business Review,* May 7, 2015, https://hbr.org/2015/05/why-compassion-is-a-better-managerial-tactic-than-toughness.

Chapter 29. Kindness and Vulnerability

1. Brené Brown, "The Power of Vulnerability," TED Talk, recorded June 2010 at TEDxHouston, 20:13, https://www.ted.com/talks/brene_brown_on_vulnerability.
2. Brené Brown, *The Power of Vulnerability: Teachings on Authenticity, Connection, and Courage* (Boulder, CO: Sounds True, 2013), audiobook.
3. Brené Brown, "The Power of Vulnerability," TED Talk, recorded June 2010 at TEDxHouston, 20:13, https://www.ted.com/talks/brene_brown_on_vulnerability.

Chapter 30. Choosing to Be For or Against

1. Jerry Large, "Snohomish Woman's Heartfelt Decision about Young Life," *Seattle Times,* June 4, 2015, http://www.seattletimes.com/seattle-news/tears-mix-with-snohomish-womans-heartfelt-decision/.

Chapter 31. What Do You Want Your Legacy to Be?

1. David Brooks, The Road to Character (New York: Random House, 2015), xi.

Chapter 32. Extending Kindness to All: Kindness Isn't Selective or Conditional

1. "Bank Loses $1 Million Deposit in Parking Validation Dispute," *Washington Post,* February 21, 1989, https://www.washingtonpost.com/archive/business/1989/02/21/bank-loses-1-million-deposit-in-parking-validation-dispute/1f5a3a42-b5aa-4857-bcc3-89579b367c58/.

Chapter 34. What Are You Looking For (Really)?

1. Wayne Muller, *How, Then, Shall We Live?: Four Simple Questions That Reveal the Beauty and Meaning of Our Lives* (New York: Bantam Books, 1996), 104.
2. Anne Lamott, *Grace (Eventually): Thoughts on Faith* (New York: Riverhead Books, 2007), 117.

Chapter 35. Big Bullies

1. "Bullying Statistics: Anti-bullying Help, Facts, and More," http://www.bullyingstatistics.org/.

Chapter 36. Little Bullies: Where It All Begins

1. Jenny Hulme, *How to Create Kind Schools: 12 Extraordinary Projects Making Schools Happier and Helping Every Child Fit In* (London: UK, Jessica Kingsley Publishers, 2015).
2. Jenny Hulme, "Can You Teach Kindness?" Interview by *Psychologies,* November 13, 2015, https://www.psychologies.co.uk/can-you-teach-kindness.
3. "Kindness Matters: We Can Change the World!" http://kindness-matters.org/.

Chapter 37. Bystanding . . . or Standing Up for Kindness?

1. Philip Zimbardo, *The Lucifer Effect: Understanding How Good People Turn Evil* (New York: Random House, 2008).

2. Philip Zimbardo, quoted in "Eight Ways to Stand Up to Hate," Elizabeth Svoboda, *Greater Good*, November 22, 2016, http://greatergood.berkeley.edu/article/item/eight_ways_to_stand_up_to_hate.

3. Megan Kelley Hall & Carrie Jones, eds., *Dear Bully: Seventy Authors Tell Their Stories* (New York: HarperCollins, 2011).

4. Megan Kelley Hall, quoted in "How to Stand Up to Adult Bullies," Anna North, *Jezebel*, October 20, 2011, http://jezebel.com/5851820/how-to-stand-up-to-adult-bullies.

5. "Eyes on Bullying: What Can You Do?" www.eyesonbullying.org.

6. www.bullying.org

Chapter 38. Choosing Our Cyber-Voices and Media Companions

1. Elizabeth Svoboda, "Virtual Assault," *Scientific American Mind, November/December 2014, 46-53*

Chapter 41. What If I Don't Feel Like Being Kind?

1. Shanna Peeples, "Warriors of Kindness," *Huffington Post*, updated December 6, 2017; http://www.huffingtonpost.com/shanna-peeples/warriors-of-kindness_b_8258882.html.

2. Ann Macfarlane, "Avoiding Amygdala Hijack," *Jurassic Parliament*, September 3, 2015, https://www.jurassicparliament.com/avoiding-amygdala-hijack/.

3. Peggy Drexler, "Why We Love to Gossip," *Psychology Today*, August 12, 2014, https://www.psychologytoday.com/blog/our-gender-ourselves/201408/why-we-love-gossip.

Chapter 46. What We Want Most for Our Kids

1. Kathryn E. Buchanan and Anat Bardi, "Acts of Kindness and Acts of Novelty Affect Life Satisfaction," *Journal of Social*

Psychology 150, no. 3 (August 2010): 235–37, https://doi.org/10.1080/00224540903365554.

2. "The Social Capital Community Benchmark Survey," John F. Kennedy School of Government, Harvard University, https://sites.hks.harvard.edu/saguaro/communitysurvey/results.html.

3. Sonja Lyubomirsky, "Almost Any Types of Acts of Kindness Boost Happiness," interview by Gretchen Rubin of The Happiness Project, *Psychology Today*, January 18, 2013, https://www.psychologytoday.com/blog/the-happiness-project/201301/almost-any-types-acts-kindness-boost-happiness.

4. Sonja Lyubomirsky, "The Myths of Happiness," interview by Woopaah, September 21, 2013, http://www.woopaah.com/blog/2013/9/21/the-myths-of-happiness-an-interview-with-sonja-lyubomirsky.html.

5. Emma Seppälä, "How to Apply the Science of Happiness to Accelerate Your Success," Stanford Medicine, The Center for Compassion and Altruism Research and Education, January 15, 2016, http://ccare.stanford.edu/?s=%22self-criticism+is+basically+self-sabotage%22.

6. Sarah-Joyce Battersby, "Kindness Tops List of What Parents Hope to Teach Kids, Forum Poll Finds," *Toronto Star*, January 1, 2016, https://www.thestar.com/news/gta/2016/01/01/cool-to-be-kind-forum-poll.html.

7. Amy Joyce, "Are You Raising Nice Kids? A Harvard Psychologist Gives 5 Ways to Raise Them to Be Kind," *Washington Post*, July 18, 2014, https://www.washingtonpost.com/news/parenting/wp/2014/07/18/are-you-raising-nice-kids-a-harvard-psychologist-gives-5-ways-to-raise-them-to-be-kind/.

Chapter 48. Strategies for Bringing Kindness into our Life

1. Juliana Breines, "Three Strategies for Bringing More Kindness into Your Life," *Greater Good*, September 16,

2015, http://greatergood.berkeley.edu/article/item/three_strategies_for_bringing_more_kindness_into_your_life.

Chapter 50. A Dozen Reasons to Choose Kindness

1. Christopher M. Barnes, "Sleep-Deprived People Are More Likely to Cheat," *Harvard Business Review*, May 31, 2013, https://hbr.org/2013/05/sleep-deprived-people-are-more-likely-to-cheat.

Acknowledgments

I have been blessed to have known so many kind people throughout my life and to have had a career in a field where kindness is common and widespread. Lynn Melby, my friend and business partner for more than three decades, along with his wife, Joye, are among the kindest ever to have walked the planet. My other gracious business partners, Patty Anderson and Dana Murphy-Love, were gifts beyond measure, as were the many members of our team over the years.

The colleagues and nonprofit volunteer leaders I've worked with have consistently demonstrated the value of contributing their time, talent, and treasure to improve the world—I learned from their kindness daily.

Writing is often a solitary endeavor, but certain people were always there with support and encouragement. I have been consistently energized and inspired by the talented Kristen Leathers, dear friend and writing partner. Nancy Faerber offered to be my beta reader and went even further, becoming a treasured friend; I learned so much from her sage and insightful feedback. Ditto Jerry Croft, an old friend whose publishing know-how came at exactly the right time (even if I didn't always heed his advice). My "boot camp" writing buddies, Carol Middleton, Kathi Bethell, and Lisa Newcomb, have been a consistent source of encouragement, support, and writing wisdom. One of these days, campers, we *will* connect in person—and the first round's on me!

From its inception, I met wise and wonderful people through my blog. I so appreciate everyone who followed it and especially those who took the time to comment, to engage, and to encourage me to think and explore my ideas more critically. Those who were themselves bloggers consistently inspired and entertained me with their kind and quirky perspectives. In a world where social media is often unkind, the blogging community is a welcome exception. Christine Opiela helped me set up my blog when I knew so little about WordPress that I assumed it was a new way to iron clothes. She continues to be my mentor and friend for all things technology!

Brooke Warner and her team at She Writes Press have been tremendous to work with. I am so happy that my publishing path led me to SWP. In addition to Brooke, huge thanks to project manager Cait Levin and to dynamic editorial duo Jennifer Caven and Katie Caruana for editing with an eagle's eye and a writer's ear. And to Mimi Bark and Tabitha Lahr for cover and interior design.

Working with JKS Communications as my publicist was educational, enlightening, and also enormously fun! Angelle Barbazon, Marissa DeCuir, and the JKS team consistently knocked my socks off with their creativity, their tenacity, and their kindness.

As I've gotten older, and perhaps even a bit wiser, I've seen ever more clearly what treasures my friends are—the ones I've known for decades and the ones who have come into my life only recently . . . the ones who are near, or far, or buddies through email. The extraordinary Rachel Remen—an exceedingly kind person—has said that the secret to living well is "pursuing unanswerable questions in good company." I couldn't agree more, and I thank you, my friends, for being such good company.

It has been said that kindness begins at home, and I have my parents, Walter and Connie Cameron, to thank for teaching me to love words and showing me the importance of kindness. They are long gone, but my talented sister, Kim, continues to encourage and surprise me. And, of course, Bill—I hit the jackpot with you, my love. Thank you for taking seriously that wedding vow I slipped in that you must make me laugh every day. You haven't missed yet!

About the Author

Donna Cameron has spent her career working with non-profit organizations and causes—as an executive, consultant, trainer, and volunteer. She has seen kindness in action and been awed by its power to transform. When she committed to a year of living kindly she considered herself a reasonably nice person (with occasional lapses into bitchiness), but she knew that true kindness was a step above—and over the course of that year, she learned that it takes practice, patience, and understanding . . . not to mention a sense of humor. The recipient of multiple writing awards, Cameron has published numerous articles and, in 2011, coauthored (with Kristen Leathers) *One Hill, Many Voices: Stories of Hope and Healing.* Raised in the San Francisco Bay Area, Donna now lives in a suburb of Seattle with her husband.

Author photo © Bill Wiederkehr

Selected Titles From She Writes Press

She Writes Press is an independent publishing company
founded to serve women writers everywhere.
Visit us at www.shewritespress.com.

Note to Self: A Seven-Step Path to Gratitude and Growth
by Laurie Buchanan. $16.95, 978-1-63152-113-3. Transforming
intention into action, *Note to Self* equips you to shed your baggage,
bridging the gap between where you are and where you want to
be—body, mind, and spirit—and empowering you to step into
joy-filled living *now!*

Think Better. Live Better. 5 Steps to Create the Life You Deserve
by Francine Huss. $16.95, 978-1-938314-66-7. With the help of this
guide, readers will learn to cultivate more creative thoughts, realign
their mindset, and gain a new perspective on life.

*This Way Up: Seven Tools for Unleashing Your Creative
Self and Transforming Your Life* by Patti Clark. $16.95, 978-
1-63152-028-0. A story of healing for women who yearn to lead
a fuller life, accompanied by a workbook designed to help readers
work through personal challenges, discover new inspiration, and
harness their creative power.

*Stop Giving it Away: How to Stop Self-Sacrificing and Start
Claiming Your Space, Power, and Happiness* by Cherilynn
Veland. $16.95, 978-1-63152-958-0. An empowering guide de-
signed to help women break free from the trappings of the needs,
wants, and whims of other people—and the self-imposed limita-
tions that are keeping them from happiness.

*Where Have I Been All My Life? A Journey Toward Love
and Wholeness* by Cheryl Rice. $16.95, 978-1-63152-917-7.
Rice's universally relatable story of how her mother's sudden
death launched her on a journey into the deepest parts of grief—
and, ultimately, toward love and wholeness.

Body 2.0: Finding My Edge Through Loss and Mastectomy
by Krista Hammerbacher Haapala. An authentic, inspiring guide
to reframing adversity that provides a new perspective on preven-
tative mastectomy, told through the lens of the author's personal
experience.

.